PLAIN EDUCATIONAL TALKS.

Plain Educational Talks

WITH

TEACHERS AND PARENTS.

BY

ALBERT N. RAUB, A. M.,
SUPT. OF LOCK HAVEN PUBLIC SCHOOLS.

PHILADELPHIA:
CLAXTON, REMSEN & HAFFELFINGER,
819 and 821 Market Street.
1869.

STEREOTYPED BY J. FAGAN & SON. PRINTED BY MOORE BROS.

TO

My Beloved Wife,

WHOSE READY SYMPATHY, WARM ENCOURAGEMENT, AND
EARNEST PRAYERS, HAVE BEEN MY
CONSTANT SUPPORT,

I Dedicate this Volume

AS

A TOKEN OF AFFECTION.

PREFACE.

IN a number of instances during the past few years, I have been requested to furnish my educational lectures for publication. I have steadily refused complying with all such requests from time to time, but have at length, at the solicitation of my friends, embraced much of the matter in the following chapters. This must be my apology for bringing before the public another work on the subject of which this book treats. Yet the subject is so important in all its bearings, and of such vital interest, that too much can hardly be said on it, and it may be, therefore, that no apology is needed.

One object in view in the preparation of this work has been to produce such a book as would recommend itself by the variety of topics, and the manner in which they are discussed, to the attention of both teachers and parents. In order to accomplish this it has been divested as much as possible of the didactic character which all educational works in a certain measure must assume. It is not meant to be a scientific treatise at all, but simply, what its title indicates, *Plain Educational Talks with Teachers and Parents.* The subject is a broad one, and of course in a volume the size of this its treatment cannot be comprehensive.

My greatest ambition in the preparation of this volume, which has been written almost wholly during the spare evening hours of a hard winter's work, has been to present a book which the thoughtful teacher or parent may read through with interest, and when he comes to lay it down, be able and willing to say: "There are some good ideas in it; it is worth reading." If I have succeeded in my object, I shall feel grateful, not only that I was led to undertake the work, but that my success has exceeded my expectations.

I have adopted a simple style, aiming at neither rhetorical display nor scientific technicality. I deemed this necessary because I prepared the volume for both parents and teachers; and having a plain subject to talk about and some plain things to say, I have tried to say them in such a plain way that every one can understand. The book differs from most other educational works in this particular, and it may, therefore, provoke criticism. It is hoped, however, that the end aimed at will protect it from any unprovoked assaults.

I have tried to say in this book what I have said frequently before large bodies of teachers and parents throughout my own State, and should this waif be welcomed and as cordially received as has been its author on the occasions referred to, I feel that I have nothing to fear. I therefore commend the volume to the kindly consideration of the parents and teachers of this country, hoping that it will be kindly received and that the practical hints contained in it, though given in a homely and familiar way, may serve to awaken thought and arouse greater interest in the true development of the children of the land, and at the same time prove an acceptable addition to that educational literature of the country which has already done so much towards elevating our condition and adding to our improvement as a race.

A. N. R.

LOCK HAVEN, PA., *June* 1, 1869.

CONTENTS.

CHAPTER XII.

CHAPTER XIII.

CHAPTER XIV.

CHAPTER XV.

CHAPTER XVI.

CHAPTER XVII.

CHAPTER XVIII.

CHAPTER XIX.

CHAPTER XX.

CHAPTER XXI.

PLAIN EDUCATIONAL TALKS.

CHAPTER I.

WHAT IS TRUE EDUCATION?

PROBABLY no more important question than this has ever claimed attention. Its importance, too, makes it one to which it is difficult to give a satisfactory answer. Education, in its true sense, seems to be a full, perfect discipline, not only of the mental and moral powers, but of the physical as well. Man, in his dual nature, cannot be trained perfectly by developing alone either the body or the soul. A training purely physical makes him a mere brute, and lowers him to the brute's level; and, on the other hand, a training which is wholly devoted to mind makes him weak, imbecile, helpless as a babe, and is, in the end, but little better than training purely physical. We have no respect for those brutish men who lack both culture and knowledge. Their manner, to say nothing of their conduct, is so utterly at variance with our feelings, that we are forced to abhor and despise them. But what is our treatment of those equally one-sided men whose culture has been purely that of mind? Are they not our demi-gods? Do we not hold them up as examples for the emulation of the young? We caution our youth against misdirected education: all education is misdirected and false that tends to make man one-sided, whether it be such as is purely physical, or such as is purely mental or moral. God has not given us any powers to lie dormant. We have talents; some one, some five, some ten, and some a hundred. We dare not bury them. They were given us for improvement, and it is for us to show ourselves faithful stewards of our trust. The development of these talents must be full and perfect.

There are so many one-sided, one-idead men in this world, that one is almost led to the conclusion that our education has been all wrong. There are so many who, when placed in any other sphere than the one they now occupy, would prove utterly helpless, that we are forced to believe that much of our education has been at least sadly misdirected. Our urgent need is men and women who are something and somebody in a physical as well as in a mental or a moral sense. We need men and women who are not one-sided, weak, ill-proportioned, and unfit to do their work in the world. No nation can prosper under the rule of those but half-fitted for their work, and yet it is a lamentable fact that in our country, which aspires to the first rank among the nations of the world, we very often elevate to power men who are wholly unfit for the positions they are made to fill. Intriguing, wire-working politicians, with an eye to the spoils, select our candidates for us, and by shrewdness, and trickery, and bravado, amid the clangor of horns, the beating of drums, and the shouts of the populace, they rush them into place and power. Not fitness, but money and political influence are the forces that play the controlling part in the selection of too many of our public officers. We all feel that it should not be so, and yet we feel that unfortunately it is so.

One of the great educational problems that we are called upon to solve is just this: How shall we, in a country like ours, keep our government pure and our rulers incorrupt and uncontaminated? It is a question which is ever likely to arise in a republic, where all claim the same political privileges, and all are alike eligible to the same offices. The love of power and influence, and the greed for the emoluments of office, are so great that few possibly can resist the temptation to enter public life, and fewer still are able, when once entered, to resist the corruption of the various rings and cliques. Our education for good citizenship has been too long neglected. We are too much afraid of the politician and his influence. There are too many axes to grind. It is hard to predict the future of our nation, if we do not make an effort to mend matters. Can this government exist as a republic under the influences which now control many of its rulers? Here is a question to which it is difficult to give an answer that shall be both satisfactory and correct.

In order to educate, we must not only know how to educate, but also why we educate. First of all, we must know why. Yet there are those in this world by the thousand who think they know how, and yet know not the *why!* They study methods of instruction and methods of government, and yet know not what they intend to accomplish. They know what means to apply, and how to apply them; but they know not the end they seek. They have no ideal. The whole work is routine, call it by whatever pretty name you please. This, too, may be said of both parents and teachers.

Richter says, "If the secret variances of a large class of ordinary fathers were brought to light, and laid down as a plan of studies and reading catalogue for moral education, they would run somewhat after this fashion: In the first hour, pure morality must be read to the child, either by myself or the tutor; in the second, mixed morality, or that which may be applied to one's own advantage; in the third, 'Do you not see that your father does so and so?' in the fourth, 'You are little, and this is only fit for grown-up people;' in the fifth, 'The chief matter is that you should succeed in the world, and become something in the state;' in the sixth, 'Not the temporary, but the eternal, determines the worth of a man;' in the seventh, 'Therefore, rather suffer injustice, and be kind;' in the eighth, 'but defend yourself bravely, if any one attack you;' in the ninth, 'Do not make such a noise, dear child;' in the tenth, 'A boy must not sit so quiet;' in the eleventh, 'You must obey your parents better;' in the twelfth, 'and educate yourself.' So, by the hourly change of his principles, the father conceals their untenableness and one-sidedness. As for the wife, she is neither like him nor like that harlequin who came on to the stage with a bundle of papers under each arm, and answered to the inquiry what he had under his right arm, 'Orders,' and to what he had under his left, 'Counter-orders;' but the mother might be much better compared to a giant Briareus, who had a hundred arms, and a bundle of papers under each." American fathers and mothers, is this a picture of life? Is there not too much truth in it?

The sculptor sees in the block of marble, rough, unshapen, and cold, as it lies before him, it may be, an angel with wings of gold and clad in the vesture of heaven; or, it may be, a warrior mounted on his fire-breathing charger, wearing his coat of mail and armor of steel. To you and me the block is a huge stone, and nothing more. He has his ideal, and the incessant blows of his mallet and chisel will reveal the figure in all its grace and power. Did he not have this ideal, and see it in the marble which to us is cold and lifeless, he were no better sculptor than we. So, too, in an educational sense we must have our ideal. We must see in the future a model man or a model woman who shall be our guide. Do we labor blindly, without knowing what end we wish to accomplish or whither we are drifting, we labor to no purpose. To educate properly, then, we must first determine why we educate. We must know the end; and, knowing this, we can apply the means at hand to the end in view.

CHAPTER II.

MACHINE EDUCATION.

THIS is the age of machines. Our labor is done by machinery. An American genius puts his wits to work, and the result is a reaper which walks through our grass and grain fields, laying everything low as it sweeps along like a thing of life. We follow the grain to the barn; and lo! the farmer is his own miller. Here in his barn is a machine, a new invention, a horse-power grist-mill. In vain we sigh for the days when the reaper swung his sickle in the golden grain, or the mower his scythe in the fragrant grass. The poetry of it now exists in language only. In vain the miller dams the water: his occupation is gone, and his damming is of no avail. The old mill-wheel, with its great wooden buckets, is at last at rest, and the minnows now play fearless among the paddles. But not here alone do we find the evidence of inventive genius cropping out. Everywhere the click of the hammer and the sharp, shrill scream of the whistle, or the buzz and whirr of the busy spindle resound in our ears. We are surrounded by machines—pumping machines, planing machines, calculating machines, and at last some inventive genius starts out a huge monster man-shaped machine, with neck for steam-pipe, and chest and abdomen for boiler, and puts it in shafts and trots it down the street before our very eyes —a steam man. We look at him astounded, and, holding our breath as we dubiously survey our bodies to make sure that we too are not mere machines, we ask in a whisper, What next?

Now, I don't object to all this machine-work in its proper place. If clothes can be made in a shorter time by the aid of a sewing-machine than by hand, then let us have the sewing-machine, and feel grateful too that its inventor was an American; and if the work on the farm can be done better and more quickly by improved machinery than by the old methods, and there is no doubt that it can, then, by all means, let us make use of all the labor-saving machinery we can get; but let us confine our machinery and machine-work to their proper place.

There is such a thing as machine education. There are those among parents and in the school-room who never for a moment give any thought to the method in which they propose to educate. Having full faith in the ability of their ancestors, they follow out the example set them, and, like the farmer who plows, and sows, and reaps, in imitation of his fathers, they seem to have no desire for any better plan. I have visited friends whose first question with reference to my children, after satisfying them as to the number, was, "Does your little girl know her letters?" or, "Does your little boy go to school?" It was taken for granted that the alphabet of our language, consisting of arbitrary characters, is necessarily the first round in the ladder of learning; and that the first thing to be done when a child is able to walk is to send it to school, to sit there on uncomfortable benches, and spend, it may be, half a winter in committing to memory a number of arbitrary signs, which, to it, have little more meaning and interest than the characters on a Chinese tea-chest or a pack of fire-crackers.

We have become so much accustomed to mere routine, traveling on in the old beaten track, and at the same old pace, for so long a time, that we scarcely know how to get out of it. But get out of it we must. The world moves, and we must move with it, lest, like other fossils, we be labeled and shelved in some antiquarian's cabinet as a curiosity, a relic of the bygone. There is a live, active, and acting present, which either hurries us along with it, or, if we hold back too persistently, drops us by the way and leaves us to ourselves. We may petrify if we desire it, or we may throw in our lot with the rest and be a living, moving, active organism. The world cares not much which. One individual is of too little significance to put a check on the energy, activity, and progress of the rest. As well might one imitate the dame in driving back the sea with her broom, as attempt to stay the progressive spirit of the age. The march is onward, and there is no retreat. The phalanx moves forward in a solid column, and there is neither obstacle nor opposition that can check its progress. Hence, I say, the man of to-day must march with it, or, if he will oppose, be thrown aside to fossilize.

But let us look at this matter from another standpoint. Which accomplishes the more good for the young, he who follows the same plan from day to day, or he who varies every day's work to suit the circumstances and the wants of the day? There is no doubt that the live, energetic teacher, whether it be the mother in her own family with her little ones gathered about her knee, or the young man or young woman who rules over a school, accomplishes infinitely more than one of that other type who takes Johnny to his knee and says, "Johnny, what's that?" and when Johnny innocently confesses his ignorance, tells him, "That's A, you blockhead!" and going on to the next, repeats the question, "Johnny, what's that?" when Johnny, being still ignorant of the names of these wonderful characters, is told, "That's B, you dunce!" and so on to Z, when Johnny is sent to his seat with the kindly admonition that he shall be a good boy and study his lesson. Such teaching is a mere farce, and were the teacher not a greater ignoramus than the child, he would abandon it. The idea of sending a child to his seat to *study* a lesson consisting of characters which have no more significance to him than so much Cherokee or Choctaw would have to you and me, is simply absurd. It were ten times better for the child to be out at play, building houses of corncobs or ovens of sand moulded over its own bare, brown foot as a support to the arch. There can be no question in the mind of any intelligent person as to which of these teachers does the greater good. It is n't any wonder that very many children have a horror of books and dread going to school. Were you and I fed on the same mental pabulum and with the same spoon that some of our children are, we would sympathize with the little folks, and do something to make school-life pleasanter for them. I rather think that we would rebel against the constituted authorities. There are few of us who would sing with any feeling,

"I would I were a boy again,"

if being a boy were to bring back our earliest school-days and school experiences. For one, I feel grateful that I have at least learned the alphabet; although under the old regime, the machine-system, which, unfortunately, is still too prevalent, it did take a full winter, if not more, to initiate the pupils into the mysteries of the A, B, C.

There is, however, much of what may be called machine teaching outside of the alphabet. We find it in almost every branch taught. Have you no recollections of your teacher, who, when the reading-class was called, sat at his desk, and while you and your classmates read on in turn, "mended" some little urchin's pen or "did some sums" for some of the boys, paying no attention to his class until, suddenly looking up, he inquires, "Where are you reading?" or, hearing you halt, asks, "Charley, how many times have you read around?" and when Charley answers, "Three times, sir," replies, "That will do; take the next lesson. Go to your seats." You did go, too, in your own peculiar style. So utterly negligent have many teachers and parents been, that it is now almost an impossibility to select one good reader from every hundred persons who suppose themselves able to read. Why is this true? Because by this machine way of doing things the child has never been taught to read; all the early years of its life were spent in pronouncing words, which is all very important in itself, but then it is not reading. Reading is something more than pronunciation. Unless we give expression to the sentiment, the mere calling of words amounts to nothing. Take the trouble to listen to a class of children read, as they call it, and you will find almost all have contracted bad habits that will adhere to them to a certain extent through life. It is n't at all strange that there are so few good readers. As a general thing, the failure may always be traced back to mere routine teaching. It is not my province here to say how reading should be taught; but were I asked how to proceed, I should say, Never allow the child, from the moment it makes its first attempt to read, to do it in any other than a natural manner. Permit no whining and drawling, or stammering and halting, but see that the child is able to pronounce every word before attempting to read a line, and then let it read the selection just as you would have it talk it. If no bad habits are formed at first, there will be none in after-life to overcome.

In the same manner I might illustrate this machine teaching in all the branches taught either at home or in school; for there is just about as much of it in one place as in the other. There is not a branch, from the alphabet to Latin and Hebrew, in which you may not find it. "There is no royal road to learning" is an old proverb, and the student realizes the truth of it when he enters upon school-life. But though the road may not be royal, there is no necessity for its being the contrary. It may be necessary to administer some hard knocks, as has been said, but it does seem to me as if too much of education has heretofore consisted of these hard knocks, and too little in pleasure. The danger does not lie so much in the direction of making study too easy as it does in the opposite one, and hence arises, and is supported, this routine system of teaching, which does so much toward making mere parrots of our children.

One of the peculiar ideas of this fossilized system is, that pupils must necessarily remain in school six hours each day. Can you imagine yourself in greater agony than to be required for six hours in a day, five days in the week, throughout the whole of eight or ten years, to sit in an erect position on a bench from which you are unable to touch the floor with your feet? It seems to me that if an attempt were made to devise some plan of torture, we could hit upon nothing better than to place the victim on one of these high benches six hours a day with nothing to do and nothing to read, unless it be a Hindoo grammar printed wholly in the original. Neither you nor I would like such treatment. Yet we think it all right when we subject our children to the same sort of treatment and for the same length of time. Public opinion, which is based on the parent's convenience and not on the child's welfare, I know, says that pupils should be kept in six hours; but public opinion, at least so far as primary schools are concerned, is wrong. The only thing accomplished by such protracted sessions is, that the children are kept out of the way of the folks at home.

It seems, however, a little like unchristian benevolence to prejudice the bodily health of a child for the convenience of the parent. That many diseases are engendered in the school-room — to say nothing of deformed spines and contracted chests — is a fact that is beyond denial. Really too little attention has been paid to the physical health and comfort of the child. Parents do their child a great wrong in confining it in the school-room so long a time, when, in reality, the position it often assumes and the air it is compelled to breathe are both detrimental to health. The idea that the child is studying or at work is erroneous. It does not know how to study; and all the time beyond two or three hours that it is required to keep its seat, is worse than wasted. It isn't any wonder at all that the children in our primary schools are usually more noisy than those in other schools, nor that they will amuse themselves by tormenting their neighbors or throwing spitballs at one another. It is n't their natural or normal condition to remain as motionless and stiff as statues. They had far better be at home or in the fields half of the time they are usually required to be in school. It would be more conducive to health, and "going to school" would not be so unpleasant.

Great, however, as is the number of those who fall into the errors, a few of which I have attempted to point out, there are still many noble men and women, teachers and parents, who are waking up to the importance of breaking down all systems that tend to make mere machines or toys of the young. There are many who have been finding out gradually the secret of success. Parents are waking up to the importance of doing more for their children, and we may yet see the day when children shall not be sent to school to get them out of the way at home. It seems to me that there is a brighter day ahead for us all. I know we are now groping wildly in the dark, but we shall soon be ushered into the light of high noon. But let us not suppose that we are already victorious. We have much to accomplish ere we can rest and let our boat glide with the current.

There are still too many who feel that their whole duty is done when they put the machinery in motion. These must either work according to nature's plain teachings, or they must fail. When nature dictates play to the child, or the cultivation of its perceptive faculties, it is not for these machine-men to put it to the study of the alphabet or abstract definitions. When nature plainly indicates that it is neither beneficial nor healthy to sit in a cramped or even an erect position in an ill-ventilated room, it is not for one of these wiseacres to quarrel with her by trying to make statues of children, and, at the same time, implant the seeds of future mental and physical disease along with the alphabet and all the other mysteries of his erudition.

There is a sad need that public sentiment be modified; and, instead of taking for granted that we have always been right in our theories, we should investigate them, and make an earnest effort to do away with everything that is mere routine.

CHAPTER III.

EDUCATIONAL CRAMMING.

WHEN a lad at thirteen years of age, I was so unfortunate as to have studied, in a common country school, in addition to the ordinary common branches of education, Algebra, Mensuration, Physiology, Natural Philosophy, Chemistry, Physics, Watts on the Mind, Moral Science, History, Rhetoric, Botany, Etymology, and some German. I was, of course, represented to my parents by the teacher as being a smart lad, although I knew nothing, comparatively, of any of these sciences a year after having studied them. I have the satisfaction of knowing, however, that I had a number of classmates and a teacher who were my partners in ignorance. I cannot express my regret in words for my loss of time while pursuing these studies, nor for the utter stupidity of my teachers. I cannot conceive how a man can be so blind to the interests of the young as to permit himself to make so great a mistake. Goldsmith's schoolmaster was in some respects, I often think, a fair sample of the one to whose guiding care and control I was subjected in my boyhood days.

That old-style race of pedagogues has not, by any means, become extinct yet. If you take the trouble to search, you will find many a one posted behind his great desk in his easy-chair, dealing out alternately his learning and his muscle, in the same style and with the same force as twenty or more years ago, when you and I were schoolboys together. His blows, however, are not more lavishly given than his knowledge. His pupils are taught soon to put away the study of the common branches as unworthy of further notice, and turn their attention to such higher subjects as the sciences, rhetoric, and possibly French and Latin. Oh! it has sometimes made my heart ache to see one of these little fellows trudging along with a huge lexicon under one arm, and a half-dozen text-books on other subjects, in his book-strap. I was n't surprised at all when I saw his pale, waxen face, and delicate, trembling, powerless fingers. Not only his language, but his body too, has almost been given to the dead. I have thought sometimes that those of our children who attend these cramming-schools — I know no other name for them — are much in the predicament of Gulliver when carried to the house-top and fed with nauseating food by the huge Brobdignagian monkey. The only difference seems to lie in the fact that the child, instead of being helped out of its misery by its parents — who should take most interest in its welfare — is by them dragged or forced into the presence of this man-monkey, where the cramming operation is performed to its evident disgust, but to their extreme satisfaction and pleasure. We commiserate the condition of Gulliver; but Gulliver's lot was no more unhappy than is that of many a one of our children, which is mentally crammed and gorged until nature rebels against the harsh and inhuman treatment, and either removes it from our uncharitable world, or so weakens its physical system as to prevent further torture.

Parents, too, as I have said before, help to make the matter worse, by indorsing, either directly or indirectly, this system of cramming. They send their children to school, and complain bitterly if they do not progress rapidly from book to book. They seem to think that a child makes no progress unless it be advanced at such a rate as requires it to take up a new study almost every six months. Here is where much of the difficulty lies. So long as parents sanction work of this kind, we will have it. Now their duty, and the duty of every thoughtful, conscientious teacher with regard to it, seems to be plain. The mind is not only not strengthened, but it is positively weakened by an over-amount of knowledge, and it cannot perform its proper functions any more than can the stomach when too great an amount of food is repeatedly taken. In either case dyspepsia is the result: for there is such a thing as mental dyspepsia, as well as that under which those who injudiciously pamper their appetite labor. I know "it sounds big" — to use a homely phrase — to have one's child say that he has studied Latin, and possibly Geometry, Chemistry, and others of the more difficult sciences; but then the injury does more than overbalance our pride. I have now and then met parents, in my career as a teacher, who, in placing their child in my care, told me how much their boy or girl had studied, naming so many branches sometimes, that I felt like telling them I feared I could do the child no good, as it seemed to me, if there were any foundation laid, that probably the child knew more than its teachers. Let me say, however, that there is no cause for alarm. These same children never know one-fifth as much as their fond parents think they know. Their ability is usually much overrated, and their parents have been deceived as to the real amount of their knowledge. Parents, however, can blame no one but themselves for the deception; for in nine cases out of ten they have courted this very deception by urging the teacher to rush the child from book to book and from study to study at such a rate as to prevent anything like thoroughness in any subject.

Is the teacher free from censure in this matter? It is difficult at times to resist the pleadings of parents, and yet I think that, if some time were taken to argue the matter with them, setting the danger and the evil before them in the proper light, much might be done toward correcting any wrong impressions under which they may labor. It is, at least, worthy of a trial. I know many argue that parents are unreasonable. Such is not the case. Were the teacher to go to the parent, and represent the truth as it is, in the great majority of cases he would find that he has done the parents a great wrong in supposing them inclined to be unreasonable. They are interested in the welfare of their children, and they will be glad to consult with the teacher on anything that may be either for the benefit or to the interest of these little ones. I believe it to be duty of the teacher to make every effort in his power to show parents the evils arising from this forcing system.

This cramming and forcing may be compared to the work of our horticultural forcing-pits. So long as you can co-operate with nature, and give your charge the proper airing every day, the plant flourishes, but its growth is not that which will fit it for future usefulness in the outer world. Its growth is a sickly growth; although it may be vigorous, it is nevertheless pale and tender, and as a hot-house plant, in this paleness and tenderness consists most of its usefulness. When the horticulturist wishes to prepare his plants for the outer world, he does not give them this forced culture and then immediately transplant them; but first takes every precaution to harden them, so that they may be prepared to endure the more rugged and changeable atmosphere in which their future life is to be spent. He knows that if he were to transplant one of these overgrown tenderlings, almost certain destruction would be its doom. They are not prepared to endure any other atmosphere than the one in which they have been reared. The same is true as regards children. Let them be crammed with knowledge, and their culture forced, and they will be like the overgrown, weak, and brittle plant, fresh from the hot-house or forcing-pit, totally unfit to be transplanted to the cold and chilling atmosphere of the world. They have not been hardened; their mental growth has been too rapid.

You have noticed before now one of those tall, overgrown boys, lean, lank, and slender, who seem to have sprung up with almost railway speed. In vain anxious and careful mothers have attempted to make their clothing keep pace with the lengthening-out process, by making sundry additions to both coat-sleeves and pantaloons. They can't keep up. Nature is bound to keep in advance, and the young man's limbs travel ahead, and he stalks around the very picture of awkwardness. One is almost forced to smile as he notices his ungainly movements, and yet he is no more awkward than are those whose mental growth has been too rapid. Neither one has been a healthy development, and we have no confidence in the ability of either to accomplish anything. The one is too weak with all his size, and too awkward. His strength has not only not kept pace with his increased growth, but, on the contrary, it has actually diminished, and he has accomplished far less than one of the same age who is much smaller, but whose growth has been gradual. What is true in the case of bodily development is also true in mental development. No pupil that grows up under this cramming can be developed symmetrically and healthfully. You might as well attempt to controvert nature's plans in bodily development as in mental. The task is no more difficult in one case than in the other.

The organs of nutrition can assimilate only a certain amount of food and convert it into those elements which go to make up the physical part of our organism. All that is taken into the stomach beyond this is worse than superfluous, as in the end it weakens the digestive organs and is sure to breed some bodily ill. The mind, too, can make use only of that knowledge which it can retain, and nothing more. All beyond this is worthless. We may put a child to poring over Latin, and Greek, and Hebrew; or we may put it to studying, as we call it, a number of the physical sciences, and yet in the end it may know comparatively nothing, because there has been no real thinking, and none of this mental food has been assimilated. But admitting that thought has been evolved and that the mind has been disciplined, there is yet nothing gained by giving the mind an over-amount of work, as it has its allotted portion, and it will make use of no more.

It is not alone, however, in the number of studies that this cramming is practised. It is frequently in the amount of useless facts and details that are taught. I have seen those who, it appeared to me, were walking cyclopedias in some branches, and yet seemed to know just nothing of the practical affairs of life, or of many studies differing in character from those in which they seemed to be particularly erudite. I have now and then encountered walking chronological tables, who were able to name the date of every event in the world's history, and yet were unable to compute the interest on a promissory note for any number of days. I have seen pupils, too, who were stuffed so full of geographical facts — the length of every little river, the population and exact location of every little town — that one was made to think they scarcely could contain any more; and yet these little fellows could n't begin to tell why we breathe, why we ventilate our rooms, and a thousand other facts of daily importance.

It does seem to me that a lifetime is too short to waste many hours in acquiring such knowledge as is unimportant and useless either as practical or disciplinary. Teachers and parents must feel a greater interest in the real welfare of the young, and work together to prevent the injury done by this forced culture. The work needs strong wills and sympathetic hearts; with these, success is certain.

CHAPTER IV.

FASHIONABLE EDUCATION.

CLOSELY allied to the cramming referred to in the last chapter, and an equally great mistake, is what may be known as fashionable education. I speak now specially of that sort of education which is designed mainly to furnish what are falsely known as the accomplishments of life; those little politenesses which are destined to make one shine in society, which prepare young men to play the part of a coxcomb or a fop, and young women to flirt or catch a beau. Of course no one acknowledges this as the intended aim of this sort of education, but, argue as we may to quiet our consciences, it is the real end aimed at, though we give it a pleasanter and more captivating name.

Among the studies usually occupying a prominent place in the curriculum of most of our fashionable schools, are Drawing, Painting, and French. No one objects to the study of any of these, when pursued either for the discipline they may afford or for their own inherent value. An important question, however, arises here. What object is aimed at by the great majority of those who take up at least a part of these studies? Why does the young lady pay forty or fifty dollars a year for instruction in painting? Does she expect to become her own artist, or does she practise merely while her school-days last, and while she has the assistance of a teacher to put on the finishing touches, while she may be said to do the daubing? What does she propose to do with her knowledge of drawing? Does she study for the purpose of disciplining both hand and mind, or that she may make a practical application of her knowledge and skill in the future? What does she aim at in her French? Does she study it that she may be able to read it or speak it with fluency, or does she pursue the study only that she may be enabled to say that she has studied this language? I make no direct answer to these questions. I can give no answer that would satisfy me. I confess that I am compelled, from what I know of the matter, to think that the motives which lead to the study of these branches, in many cases, in some of the most fashionable schools, are not always the highest.

I would not be understood as opposing their study in any institution. I know there are those who will be glad to catch up my words here, and represent that I am narrow in my views and oppose the study of these branches; but such misrepresent me. Each of these branches is valuable in its place, and, when properly taught, no one esteems their value more highly than I. But as they are frequently studied, it is worse than time wasted. I have often felt, when examining the sketch-book of a young lady just fresh from boarding-school, where she had taken an ordinary course in painting and drawing, that I would like to put this plain question in a plain way: How many of these have you executed without the aid of a teacher? How many of them have not received the touch of another's pencil? Yet I have felt too that I would rather not hear the answer. It is a sad truth that teachers often do too much of the work themselves, and the pupil too little. I have known a teacher to go so far as to run over all the drawings of a graduating class and touch them up before submitting them to the examination of the public. You agree with me, of course, in condemning such action as dishonest in the teacher; but then that does n't stop it. We need to expose it. You ask some of these same young men or young women to sketch for you a favorite landscape, or, it may be, your own home. They confess their ignorance, by telling you that they were never taught to draw from nature; nay, worse than this, they scarcely can draw from a copy without the aid of a teacher to do the shading. What I have said of drawing is also, in a great measure, true of painting.

Let us turn our attention to some of the other studies; for painting, drawing, and French are not the only ones that enter into the fashionable course of our most fashionable schools. There are others that are made purely ornamental from the defective manner in which they are taught. Botany is one of these. The manner in which this delightful science is sometimes taught, makes the study of it almost a farce. It would probably be safe to say that nine-tenths of all those who study it according to the fashionable method, never know anything of the practical part of it. They come home after having finished the course, and are unable to make any use of their knowledge of this science, simply because they know nothing of its useful part. One would be safe in saying, that not a few of them would be unable to point out and name a half-dozen different sorts of our native forest-trees; many of them would fail to tell a field of wheat from one of rye, and be unable to distinguish the difference between the two. This knowledge in itself may not be all-important — I lay no such claims for it; and yet it must be acknowledged that this, with all other practical knowledge of the kind, is of much greater importance than knowing the Latin for the various orders and sub-orders, genera and species of the different members of the vegetable kingdom, and much else which is of no value to any one except the florist, the botanist, or the medical man. There are many facts in botany which, to the farmer, the teacher, the gardener — in fact, to every one who possesses the smallest plot of ground, or even a pot of plants in the window — are of such vast importance that there can be no excuse for omitting them, and spending time, which of right belongs to them, on something less useful. I refer especially to all that part of botany that may be applied in horticulture, arboriculture, and agriculture. There is much that may be applied by every one even in the culture of the commonest plants and flowers. There can be no objections to the study of botany when properly taught. There are few studies, in fact, which play a more important part in the every-day affairs of life than botany, and, when properly taught, it is also one of the most interesting of sciences. I object only to the manner in which it is too frequently neglected, and a mere smattering of it given to the pupil; and I make the same objection to a fashionable negligence in the case of all other studies.

One great fault of fashionable education is, that it neglects the useful for the ornamental. Were the main end of education the preparation of the young for the social circle, the ball-room, or the parlor, the ornamental might lay claims to precedence. Even then, however, a system of education that would ignore the principles of those sciences which form the groundwork of all knowledge, would be justly condemned. If this be true in the case of an education which is ornamental, what sentence shall be passed on that training which ignores the useful and practical in these times, when the true end of education is acknowledged to be something beyond mere ornament and show? Humboldt says that an Orinoco Indian, though regardless of bodily comfort, will yet labor for a fortnight to purchase paint enough to make himself admired. The Indians of our own Western wilds care more for a few gaudy trinkets than all the comforts we prize most. Such is the case with all the uncultured and savage tribes of the earth. The ornamental precedes the useful, and, strange to say, there is a tendency in the same direction in matters of mental acquisition. The object of sending our sons and daughters to boarding-school seems to be not so much to acquire useful knowledge as to acquire that which will enable them to shine in society. The young lady studies French, Spanish, or Italian, not because she hopes to make any use of these in after-life, but either because the course requires it or because it is deemed lady-like to have studied them. Other reasons, of course, are given; but are they the true ones? In many of our most fashionable establishments a great part of the time is devoted to these accomplishments, and, after all their drill in deportment, etiquette, &c., the young men and women come home with few of the real accomplishments of life! Instead of having mastered a good style of English composition, their time has been spent in learning an Italian operatic song. Instead of learning to read gracefully and with expression their own mother-tongue, they have been learning to pronounce — not read, mark you — a few French phrases. In the arts, too, the ornamental is made to take the place of the useful. Many a young woman comes away from these institutions skilled in all the mysteries of ornamental needle-work, who is n't able, when she marries, to sew on her husband's shirt-buttons respectably or make a neat button-hole in the garment of one of her little ones. So far as the practical affairs of life are concerned, or such knowledge as may be made useful in life, she is no wiser than she was the day she entered the institution. There may be exceptions — doubtless there are; but still too few. The useful has been ignored or merely made subservient to ornament. Many studies are taken up, not because any benefit is expected from them, but because they are considered essential in a fashionable education, and the young man or the young woman would be ashamed in company to confess ignorance in any of these fashionable branches, just as one of the savages would be ashamed to be seen unpainted, though he would have no hesitation in going out before the world unclothed! How much more good sense do we display than the savage? With him the ornamental precedes the useful; with us the same is true, save that in our case it is true of both body and mind, whereas in his case it is true of the body alone.

The objection urged by some against all education, that it tends to make their sons and daughters proud and too lazy to work, though not true in general, may, with a good show of justice, be urged against fashionable education. There is no doubt of it, that an ornamental education has a tendency to make young men and women hate work, not because they are lazy, but because their pride does not permit them to work. Somehow they get an idea that labor of any kind is degrading. Young man, the Paddy on the turnpike who honestly and soberly earns every penny that is paid him, may be more of a man than you are, though you may despise him because he is forced to toil for the support of his family! A friend who possesses a goodly share of the world's riches said to me one day in the presence of several of his daughters, that if he had a dozen of them, he would insist on all being as good cooks as their mother before they left the family hearth; and the mother was one of the most skillful. I felt glad to know that his daughters cheerfully supported him in his decision. To say the best of any system of education the tendency of which is to make people despise work, it is mischievous. It is true that sometimes young men return from some distant school, and have not only apparently forgotten how to work, but affect to despise the laborer. A young man of this kind who is good to drive fast horses is generally a fast youth himself, and too often not good for anything else. The young woman, too, who, in her absence at some hall, establishment, or seminary, has forgotten all about her household duties, is nothing but a mere plaything, a doll, and unfit to be the wife of any young man that expects his household to be governed by its proper mistress. An industrious, energetic young man does n't want such a woman for a wife. He can't afford to marry one woman to preside over his parlor and hire another to superintend his household. It would be useless to deny that the tendency of fashionable education is to make our boys and girls proud, arrogant, and lazy. The cause of education in general, has to shoulder the blame, whereas it should be laid to a fashionable or ornamental education alone.

Aside from the tendency to create the sentiment that labor is degrading, fashionable education tends to puff up with vanity and pride. Many a young man, the pride of his neighborhood, returns from the academy and seems to have forgotten all his old associates, save, of course, those who move in the highest circles. The same is true of the young woman who has been fashionably educated. She forgets her nearest neighbors, and is, of course, justly censured as being proud and vain. It may not be the design of any educational institution to foster a sentiment of this kind, but certainly some are liable to censure in this matter. Mothers and fathers have a disposition to show off the accomplishments of their darlings on their return home after having "finished their education," and this "but adds fuel to the flame." True, sometimes they have very little to make an exhibition of, but then that little serves to gratify the vanity of parents. The flattery of teachers having made them proud and vain, the approbation of the parents but serves to establish the fault. I believe that the man who has not a good opinion of his abilities, accomplishes little in the world. Such a candid confession may startle the reader a little, but let me add that I believe too that to have a good opinion of himself, he must have something upon which to base that opinion. It would be folly to argue that any great number of those who do thus try to show off their school training, have any substantial foundation on which to ground their claims.

A peculiarity of society in the present day, it seems to me, is that we have no boys and girls any longer above the age of twelve or fourteen. Our fashionable ideas rush them on so rapidly to manhood and womanhood, that when we seek for them beyond the age referred to, we find nothing but *young ladies* and *young gentlemen.* It is an unfortunate feature of our educational systems which destroys the natural modesty and demeanor of a child and substitutes in its stead vanity and conceit. Nothing is more unnatural and more to be dreaded than our fashionable boys and girls who have been taught to believe themselves prematurely men and women. There is something so unnatural in their conduct and in their talk, so much vanity and affectation, that one dreads to meet them. They seem to know so much, and yet know so little, that we have to pity them. Yet fond parents, blind in their affection and pride, cannot see how ridiculous their children appear in the eyes of others, but imagine them to be perfection personified.

After all, what greater ornament can society have than a man or woman who is of use to every one; one who shines no more brightly in society than at the side of the invalid's couch, or in the heart of the family? Such a man or woman is an incalculably greater ornament than the mere plaything, pretty to look at and pleasant to listen to, but of no other earthly use whatever. We need true, noble-hearted men and women in all positions of life. Let teachers, then, resist this pressure brought upon them by unthinking parents, and labor to make our education true. Let us hope that parents will no longer remain blind to the true interests of their children, in substituting that which is purely ornamental for the useful. I shall have occasion to refer again to the government to which pupils are sometimes subjected in acquiring a fashionable education, for the discipline which is practised in many institutions is no less faulty than the manner of imparting instruction.

CHAPTER V.

PRACTICAL EDUCATION.

I DO not propose here to decide what knowledge is of most value, nor what studies should be adopted as a part of the regular school course. There are, however, several questions which meet one in the outstart, that cannot be overlooked. One of these has been made the subject of the first chapter. A second is, What are the objects of an education?

Evidently, as I have tried to show in the preceding chapter, it is not preparation for society wholly, and yet this is one of the objects. Man is endowed with social instincts, and it is not his province to put them aside and wander around as a beast that tolerates no companions but its mate. The frontiersman who of choice withdraws himself from the society of his fellow-man and lives amid the wildest and most savage scenes of uncultivated nature, may claim our admiration for his bravery, but we wouldn't like to put him up as a model specimen of social life. On this question he is altogether one-sided and erratic. In truth, he knows this, and he would feel as much out of place in the social circle as you and I would among a war-party of savages. We censure, and justly too, the man or the woman who, forgetful of duty, tries to shun society. We know that God has implanted these social instincts in our nature for a noble purpose, and when we refuse to obey them, we at the same time question His wisdom. The ways of society may to us seem odd and arbitrary, or even ridiculous; if so, the greater the necessity for those who hold aloof to enter, and so change or modify its ways as to improve them. We have, however, no right to stand aloof. It is the part of education to prepare us for society; not to fit us for party-going, dancing, and much else that now takes up the time of society, but for all our duties as social beings. Whatever may tend to this end is valuable thus far as being practical.

Let it be understood here that practical education is not confined to that narrow basis which would limit it to the acquisition of such knowledge as is useful merely in acquiring riches or fame. There is a higher destiny in store for us. Some of the modern advocates of useful knowledge are possibly open to criticism for having, in their eagerness, gone too far in their censure of the culture of the past, and in their ardent advocacy of what they style modern culture. They claim too much for themselves, and grant too little to their opponents. Education does not consist wholly in gaining and treasuring up useful and important knowledge; nor is it, on the other hand, all discipline. There is a middle ground, which seems to be the true one.

Spenser says, "How to live? that is the essential question for us;" and most of us agree with him, provided that embraces not only our present life, but the preparation also for a future. Any education which tends to ignore preparation for the future, is not only radically defective, but absolutely wrong. Of all educations or systems of education, a godless one is the worst. Among the most important activities, as Spenser calls them, are those which prepare us for society, for citizenship, for parental duties, and for heaven. We owe also special duties to ourselves, particularly in preserving the health of both body and mind, and in giving them their proper culture. A practical education must give attention to all these. To be practical, it must also be symmetrical and liberal, not one-sided and narrow. The second and fourth of these activities will be discussed hereafter.

As to the proper training of youth for the responsible position of parents so little has been said, that one scarcely knows what to say and what to leave unsaid. It seems like going by one's self into a vast wilderness. You stand so far from any associates that you feel a sense of loneliness creep over you. It would be difficult to explain why our young men and women never even hear this subject talked of in their schools. Many teachers seem to have an idea that to touch on such a subject in the school-room would be terribly disastrous. "The idea," say they indignantly, "of talking to a young lady of getting married and rearing a family of children! Why, such a step would be utterly destructive of all discipline in any institution." What authority is there for such an assertion? Why should young ladies be made deceitful by such a course of treatment as is adopted in many institutions, where the cry of "A man in the house!" would so terrify a hundred of them as to make them utterly powerless? And yet "a man in the house" a few years afterward is n't a terror to a single one of them! I can see no reason for negligence in this matter. There is n't one in a thousand of these young ladies and young gentlemen who does n't expect to be married, or who does n't look forward to marriage as the great event of life. Shall they, then, men and women grown, be intrusted with the care of children without any training as to their proper treatment, either bodily or mental? It is certain that one-half of the deaths of infants chronicled annually might be prevented if young parents understood their duty. But an important question arises. How are they to understand their duty if they are studiously prevented from knowing anything about these matters? Are we not guilty of a great wrong in thus neglecting the welfare of each succeeding generation by placing its destiny in the hands of those wholly ignorant of its wants? It is true that good old grandmothers and kindly neighbors now and then come to the relief of the young folks; but these kindly people are not always at hand, and even were they, their advice is not at all times reliable. It seems little less than criminal that we should thus through false modesty neglect this training, and indirectly be the agents of hurrying countless numbers annually into the grave, while at the same time thousands upon thousands are through the ignorance of parents so enfeebled in constitution as to make life in a measure a burden to them. The amount of ignorance with regard to diet and clothing is really alarming. Let us then see to it that our sons and daughters are not permitted to grow up in ignorance of these matters. The few writers who have attempted to draw public attention to this mistake in our system of education, deserve not a little praise. Yet there are those who are inclined to call them utilitarian. Would that we had more of this utilitarianism. It is a good thing.

No one in the present day would deny that much might be done in the way of ministering more faithfully to our bodily wants. We owe it to ourselves and to those dependent upon us, to make due efforts for the preservation of both health and life. We cannot deny the necessity of acquiring the means of living; and yet, practically, in our school-life, we ignore the fact that the youth of the present will be required to take the places of their fathers, a few years hence, in business, as well as in governmental affairs. A practical education should give at least some attention to the preparation of the young for their future career as successful business-men. It is too often the case that the young man starts out in business without the remotest idea of what he expects to accomplish, and without having had any training for the actual duties and necessities of life. Happily, that part of the training which has special reference to the preservation of the body, is gained early in life through the instincts of nature. "The burnt child dreads the fire" is an old proverb, which is no less true in its figurative than in its literal sense. The mother, too, is ever watchful of her little charge, and protects it from harm and danger, when in her power to do so. But many of the laws relative to the preservation of health, of which I shall speak hereafter, must be taught either by the parent or by the teacher. The formation of habits injurious to health, which have ruined probably three-fourths of the whole civilized race, must be prevented. Nature is prompt in her warnings, but, unfortunately, men are not prompt to obey them. Sometimes the misery is so great in the case of cold, hunger, etc., that we cannot resist; but in the case of weariness of brain or body we are apt to give little heed to the warnings of nature. So also in the case of eating, drinking, and ill-ventilation. Nature here, as in the case of cold and hunger, does her part in warning us of the danger; but deeming ourselves wiser than nature, or failing from want of training to understand our duty, we take our own course, and necessarily are compelled to suffer.

Aside from the knowledge which directly tends to the preservation of health, such knowledge and training as will prove useful in earning a livelihood should form a part of every one's education. That this is necessary almost every one is ready to admit, and yet, strange to say, until within the past few years nothing has been done toward the preparation of the young in this respect. Business colleges have laid claims to imparting the instruction necessary, but they do the work only partially; for it consists of more than a knowledge of arithmetic and its applications. Most of this knowledge and training is acquired after school-life is over. The school of life imparts it, and a valuable school it is; but we would be able to enter a much higher class were we better fitted in the preparatory institution of either home or school. We have too little training in these matters. I have met with but one educator who ever confessed to having given his pupils instruction on their duty as to earning a livelihood in after-years, and this an old gentleman who spent his half-century in the school-room, leaving the cobbler's bench for the school-house, and quitting it only after fifty years of active and successful service.

A practical education must aim at strengthening the whole man, both body and mind. While the body is trained and strengthened for the active duties of life, the mind also must be strengthened to cope with the actual difficulties arising. Much of our education has thus far not been practical because it has not helped to strengthen the mind. Much of the instruction, too, that has been imparted to us has been of no use whatever either as a discipline or as valuable in itself; and much again that may have been valuable as a discipline, but which has no value as being useful, has simply supplanted that which both possesses an inherent value and is at the same time disciplinary. It is the general complaint of business men, and even of many professional men, that much of what they learned at school is of no future use to them, and that much which they might have studied at school had to be learned afterward. Why is this? Of all answers that I have heard, I know of none that is satisfactory. Certainly, if we can gather useful knowledge which possesses the same value as a discipline as that which is of value as a discipline only, it is folly to waste time on that which is not useful. I make no charges here against any of the studies pursued in any of our schools, but simply lay down my proposition as to the relative value of useful knowledge and that which is useless, all things being equal. Knowledge is practical only so far as it is useful or aids in strengthening and developing the mind, and the same may be said of educational training.

We look around us and see everywhere a lot of do-nothings, persons who are unable to accomplish anything in the world. Every profession and every calling is encumbered with them. Why is it? The only answer we can make is, that their education has been defective; it has not been practical. Their minds have not been properly disciplined and strengthened. It may be that they have been crammed with useless knowledge, which is stored in their mind like so much useless lumber. It may be, too, that their education has not been an education at all, but that, like so many buckets or sponges, they have passively received all that has been poured into them. This mere reception of knowledge is not education, much less is it practical education. The powers of mind and body have neither been trained nor strengthened in the process. Instruction and training must go hand in hand to give perfect development.

CHAPTER VI.

SELF-CULTURE.

MAN has within him a power of development, the immensity of which he often fails to estimate. Unlike the beasts of the field and the fowls of the air, he possesses a power which, when rightly used, makes him the noblest of God's creatures. The tiny little floweret, as it unfolds its delicate petals one by one, seems almost possessed of this same inner power of development, but it is not. The warm sunbeams gladden its little heart, and with joy it opens up its every leaf and petal that it may drink in the cheering sunshine; but it has no power beyond this. It has no higher state to prepare for. Its life of beauty is soon spent, and it is transformed into another state. It has no power of self-development. So also with the animal creation. Its members cannot rise to a higher state of being. Man differs from these. There is that within him which enables him to wield almost unlimited power. He has that within him which makes him not only superior to all other creatures, but, with culture and under favorable conditions, places him above those of his own race and nation. This power was given to man, like all his other powers, for his use, and therefore it must be developed.

A great mistake is often made by parents and teachers

in giving too much assistance to children in overcoming difficulties. The mother never thinks of carrying the young child in her arms after it is able to walk for itself. She knows too well that such a course would neither strengthen its limbs nor teach it to walk. A certain portion of this knowledge and culture must be the acquisition of the child itself. Were its mother to assist it continually in taking its food, she knows that it never would become self-dependent. As soon as possible, therefore, she allows the child to feed itself, although the little fingers and the clean table-cloth may become soiled in the process. She knows that the true method of teaching is by throwing it, in a measure, on its own resources. It makes more progress thus in a week than it would under the mother's care and instruction in a month. I have heard it related of a very celebrated naturalist, that when one of our present most learned professors became a pupil of his, the subject of the first lesson he received was a turtle, which he was ordered to take home with him and study closely. At the end of a week's time he returned to the naturalist, supposing that he was able, from a week's study, to tell all about it. Imagine his surprise when, after a few pointed questions, he was ordered to shoulder his turtle and study it another week. It did seem a little strange that the naturalist, who was receiving a large salary as the teacher of this gentleman, should give him no instruction whatever. But the turtle was studied more thoroughly than before, and the lesson proved a most valuable one in making the professor a student of nature instead of a mere recipient of the knowledge and teachings of other men. The teacher understood the true secret of acquiring knowledge.

There are, probably, few men in the world that accomplish anything, who are not what might be termed self-made. They are men who have acquired their knowledge and tact, whether in school or out of it, by their own individual effort. These are really the men who are the most successful in the world. We turn to every profession and calling in life, and we find the leaders men who have made themselves strong. They all can trace their influence and power to the fact that they were self-dependent. They were not the mere tools of their professors and teachers, nor the mere passive recipients of all knowledge that may have been poured into them. They have become strong, and become men of influence and power, only by the application of the strength already gained to overcoming greater difficulties than those heretofore surmounted. Were we to consult the world's history in all ages, we should find that in every case the leaders of the age were men whose cultnre was mainly self-culture. Don't understand here that a man must ignore schools to be self-cultured. Many of our ablest men have been subjected to the discipline of school, but they do not owe their strength to it, except so far as judicious teachers may have controlled their efforts, or directed them into a proper channel. The great men of the world have all been men of original thought.

The tendency of self-culture is to make one strong and accurate. The man of muscle knows that he may spend the greater part of a lifetime in receiving instructions how to use his power; and yet, without individual effort he knows he can accomplish nothing. So he takes up his dumb-bells, or punches his sand-bags, or takes his walk, or his row on the river, for the purpose of both disciplining and strengthening his body. The same law holds good in the acquisition of mental strength and activity. We must subject the mind also to discipline in order to strengthen it. The culture of the mind and the culture of the body are analogous, both depending upon the same principles in the strengthening process.

Self-culture makes one accurate. The earnest student who attempts to discipline his own mind feels much more confidence in his judgments, when once formed, than does he who depends wholly upon the instruction of another. The self-cultured man feels that he is becoming strengthened as he wrestles with one difficulty after another, and that he can rely on his conclusions because he arrives at each only after a close course of reasoning; while the man who depends entirely upon the help of teachers or books, never feels that he is competent to make a decision or reach a conclusion, because he cannot until he has first consulted another or his library. He does not think for himself, and never feels sure that he is correct, and is not, therefore, likely to be accurate. The self-cultured man, on the other hand, elucidates point after point, never leaving one and taking up another until he is certain that he has firmly established its predecessor. Thus he clears up all difficulties as he goes, building a sure foundation on which his superstructure may rest; and, when his work is finished, he knows too that it is complete, and accurate in detail.

Knowledge gained by one's individual effort is firmly impressed on the mind. We may read description after description of the scenery of the Hudson, and yet without a personal visit to that river to see for ourselves the splendor and magnificence of its scenery, we can form no proper conception of it; but having once seen it, or, better still, having once made a sketch of it, we never forget it. It is so impressed on the mind that it cannot be erased. We never gain so intricate and exact a knowledge of the appearance of any object or any scene as when we come to draw it or make a copy of it. The concentration of the mind on each particular feature is so close that the impression made is well-nigh indelible. It will not suffice for another to picture it either in words or in colors. These may please, but they do not give us that accurate knowledge which we desire. So in the case of all knowledge. The mind in acquiring it must fasten on to it and so concentrate its powers that a permanency of impression is guaranteed, and by virtue of the very conquest which the pupil has made the knowledge has been made more thoroughly his own, and he never forgets it; whereas that which has cost him no study, but has simply in a manner been poured into his mind, is held but for the day, and is then lost to him. Every teacher has noticed this fact, and every teacher knows the difference in the value of that knowledge gained by the pupil's own efforts and that which he acquired without any labor. I do not say that no knowledge may be imparted to the child in the shape of interesting talks or lectures. I have much faith in these; but then not all knowledge can be invested with this interest. There is much which in its nature is practically without interest, and here is just where the labor of the child must be performed. Here is where he is required to fasten his attention and concentrate his mental powers in overcoming the difficulty.

We find in consulting our own experience, that we usually value that most which has cost us the greatest amount of labor. This is so in all our worldly wealth, and it is so in our mental acquisitions. Gold and silver are valuable because they are scarce and difficult to get. Silks and broadcloths are more highly esteemed than other fabrics just as comfortable but lower in price, because they cost more, and what we pay for them, in turn requires more labor to secure. The same is true in knowledge. That which requires hard study and unflagging attention on our part, we prize more highly than that which is so easily acquired that it may become the property of every one. Were the matter reversed so that gold, silver, broadcloths, and silks were plentiful and cheap, and iron, tin, cotton, and wool as scarce as the others now are, our feelings would also change, and we would, no doubt, prefer what we now most affect to despise. The value is not always in the substance itself. The coin is the representative of a certain value, and it is made the representative because of its scarcity and the labor it costs to produce it. So in knowledge, also, that is most valued and most firmly impressed on the mind which costs us most study.

Self-gained knowledge has the advantage of possessing more interest than that which is imparted to us by others. I am not of those who would make all our books and sciences easier than they are. Some might doubtless be simplified — and, in being simplified, made more scientific — but there are few that should be made easier. Some text-books are, I know, unnecessarily hard, not from the matter they contain, but from their unfortunate arrangement of materials, or the clumsiness of expression from which the learner is unable to tell exactly what is meant. To a re-arrangement of these for the better no one could object, because it would simply be the correction of an error: nor could any one object to the simplification of science; but to make it easier, to assist the learner, is unnecessary. A mind which is not disciplined by hard work at least part of the time receives little, if any, real discipline, and is but little benefited by any false training it may have. To do all the mental work of the child, and expect it to be interested in the accumulation of knowledge in this way, were as great folly as to expect one to eat his food with the same relish when forced on him. There is a pleasure, too, in overcoming difficulties, of which the child is robbed when we do the work for him. I like the little boy who looks into your face and refuses to accept your proffered assistance when he is fast in a difficulty. Have you never noticed with what pride his eyes sparkle and how his whole frame is aglow with excitement when he gains the victory? That victory is worth more to him than all the help you could have given him. It has cost him some hard work, but he prizes the victory all the higher for that, and he has strengthened himself in gaining it. But that bright face is indicative of more than we read in it. There is more than the mere pride of conquest or joy of victory. That work has stamped itself so indelibly on the mind of the child that he never forgets how to master any other difficulty of the kind that may arise. The discipline his mind has received is invaluable. He has, too, gained not a little courage for the mastery of future and greater difficulties, which in itself is of the greatest importance in future life. De Fellenberg says, "The individual, independent activity of the pupil is of much greater importance than the ordinary busy officiousness of many who assume the office of educator."

Every one knows how much pleasanter it is to study that which is in itself interesting. There is no doubt that such knowledge is retained much longer, and is practically of more value frequently to us than that which is not interesting. Don't, my dear critic, be too hasty now to assume that I am going to take ground against any studies which may have the reputation of being dry. Such is not my intention at all. The difficulty is not that some of the branches we teach are dry and uninteresting, but we fail to make them interesting from our own lack of interest in them or through our lifeless manner of teaching. We give too much assistance to the pupil, and he sees none of the interesting part of many studies. He merely skims over the surface, gathering the scum, and when he meets with difficulties, by the mistaken kindness of his teacher he is helped over them without any effort of his own being required. Is it to be wondered at that so many of our young folks, when they finish their education, as it is said, are yet not able to accomplish anything? It is n't at all surprising. It is but the natural result of a mistaken training. "Do men gather grapes of thorns, or figs of thistles?"

There are those in the world, and their number is not small, who, when their school-life is finished, suppose that all study is done, or, as it is expressed, "their education is finished." No greater mistake could be made. School-life has closed, and the assistance of teachers is lost; but the real and true education has but commenced. The difficulty of the hardest problems met with in our algebras and arithmetics is as nothing compared with the problems which meet us at every turn in real life. Here we have not the assistance of a teacher any longer. We are thrown on our own responsibility. Alas! our training for self-support has been neglected, and we are unprepared to meet the social problems of the day, and we often fail. Whose fault is it? Where shall we lay the blame? Did our parents and teachers prevent our growing strong by carefully doing our work for us, lifting us over every difficulty as they were wont to do in our days of helpless infancy? They meant well, but they made a serious mistake. They did not permit us to become strong. We relied on them day after day for their assistance, and we became so accustomed to receiving their help that now, when we are sent adrift in the world, we are unable to guide ourselves aright. Too late we lament their misdirected kindnesses. We are compelled to endure the buffetings of fortune and make the best of our lot.

Parents and teachers, let me beg of you to think over this matter seriously before you allow yourselves to fall into the error of giving your children or pupils too much assistance. Let them do some hard work for themselves, and a good deal of it, before you attempt to help them any. Let them grow strong by overcoming difficulties for themselves. One of the greatest faults in our teaching is, that we do too much helping and too little training. We are too impatient to wait for the child to overcome difficulties for itself, and we insist too much on helping it out of its trouble. We forget that a habit of gaining knowledge for ourselves engendered in youth, will adhere to us through life. Let the child, therefore, make its start at self-culture as early as it can. It is safe to say, that when there is any possibility for it to overcome a difficulty, we do wrong in giving assistance. With proper care and by commencing at the proper time to urge this self-culture, we can make the coming generations stronger and more active and self-dependent.

CHAPTER VII.

THE OBSERVING FACULTIES.

IT is altogether a mistaken idea that culture commences with school-life. As soon as the little child opens its eyes and puts forth its hands, its mind also begins to unfold. The most important school is the family fireside. Here is where true culture begins, and here, too, is where the impressions are stamped most firmly. At the mother's knee, in the sitting-room, on the play-ground, in the nursery — everywhere the child is drinking in knowledge.

Have you ever noticed a little babe when the process of mental development has just begun? Watch it. Do you see that it never is quiet or idle for a moment when it is awake? God has made its constitution such that it must be busy. As it grows older and stronger, an uncontrollable desire to apply its strength seems to take hold of it. Does it sit quiet and contented on its mother's knee? No; that would be impossible; it must be down, prying into every nook and corner. Every imaginable object possesses a peculiar interest. As the child creeps around on the floor, it gathers knowledge constantly. While it gleans this, it is also strengthening its physical system, and its physical endurance is wonderful. As I watch one of my own little children creeping over the floor hour after hour, examining every tangible object, some for the hundredth time, I often wonder how it is possible for it to endure so much physical exertion. Yet the knowledge which it is gleaning, seems to possess so much interest and inherent entertainment that the child apparently never tires. On it goes day after day, on its hands and knees, or, it may be, bolt upright as it draws itself along by pressing its little heels into the carpet. It is the pursuit of knowledge under difficulties, it is true, but then it well repays the labor expended. Does a mother hastily remove everything from her child's reach, lest it should break something? and does she consider it troublesome or getting into all sorts of mischief? She certainly does not understand the case of her child. It is n't mischief that leads it to make these efforts to take hold of everything it can put its little hands on. The curiosity in its nature must be satisfied, and if the child cannot gratify this curiosity in one way, some other will be devised.

Culture begins, really, in advance of the child's creeping or walking period. Long before it feels the impulse in its little body to be down on the floor amusing itself and moving around, it finds something to entertain it, and from which to gather knowledge, in its mother's collar or ribbon, or in a rattle, a pencil, a stick, a knife—in fact, in anything which its little hands can hold or carry to its mouth. From this point its knowledge increases, and the process of development goes on. Day after day it adds to its store. We really fail to estimate the amount and the value of the knowledge gained by us when children under the age of eight. It possesses tenfold more importance and value than we are accustomed to place on it. What we learn previous to this period is the real groundwork of all our knowledge. It is the foundation on which we base all that follows. The acquisition of this knowledge is under the direct supervision of the parents. Has it ever occurred to you, parents, that, as your little ones are creeping around on the floor, they are gaining this knowledge? Has it ever occurred to you that there are special duties devolving upon you, as fathers and mothers, in assisting the child to glean a rich harvest? But whether you give the child the benefit of a proper supervision or not, the work goes on. It does not stop because no one directs it; it only makes mistakes now and then, and sometimes travels in a wrong direction. But the fact that the work does go on does not relieve us as parents of the responsibility of guiding and directing the infantile efforts into the proper channel.

It is, undoubtedly, the duty of parents to aid their children in acquiring knowledge, and at no time is this duty more imperative than previous to the child's entrance into school. I expect you to look surprised. Let me say to you that I am not alone in the opinion. It is the belief of those who have thought most on the subject, that much the most important period of culture is that which precedes school-life. Of course here the teacher can do nothing, and it remains for the parents, and, I may say, especially the mother, as her advantages are usually the greater, to accomplish all that is to be accomplished. Are parents prepared for the performance of this important work? I speak directly to you, parents. Do you appreciate the immensity of the task imposed upon you? Do you feel that you have the necessary preparation to perform it faithfully? I know that some parents do not have this preparation. Of course I do not expect you, however, to be among this number, because most intelligent parents have the necessary preparation, though they may not at all times feel sufficient interest in the welfare of their children to do their duty. Reader, don't think that I mean you, unless you feel guilty. If you feel guilty, however, I have no objection to your taking so much of it to yourself as you think applies in your special case. Has it never occurred to you, that the instructions of parents are of immeasurable value? Your office as instructor is really of more importance than that of the professor. Your assistance is called in when the child is acquiring such knowledge as is not found in books, really the most valuable of all knowledge. How important it is that the knowledge the child gathers be of the right kind, and that his conclusions be correct! An error imbibed at this period of life may be ever after a source of trouble. It may require years to eradicate the false knowledge gained in a single day.

It is the duty of parents to gratify the child's curiosity. You tell me that some children are so inquisitive that they are troublesome. They are forever asking questions. I am glad to hear that you have met children of this kind. I hope that you are blessed with inquisitive children. You never heard of an inquisitive child that did not or will not become somebody in the world. Give these children that are always restless, ever inquiring, "What's that for?" or "What's this made of?" a fair chance. It shows that there is an active mind there, and one that is bound to acquire knowledge if you give it a chance. You are fortunate if you have such pupils. They may cause you some trouble in the way of noise; but it is far better to have their noise than that death-like silence which is a sure indication of absolute monarchy and despotism. The teacher or the parent who repels the curiosity of children or becomes impatient under their questioning, is guilty of a great wrong. A teacher of this kind is out of place in the school-room, and a child with such parents is unfortunate, to say nothing worse. There is nothing that so much pleases the true teacher or the parent anxiously and ardently interested in his child's welfare, as to have the little one ask him questions when there is behind it all a real desire for knowledge, and the child asks simply because it does want to know. There is no affectation about its questions, as there is about those of older persons too often when they inquire of your health or the health of your family, or put some other question simply as a matter of form. The man who meets you on the street and says, "How are you?" or "How do you do?" does n't expect you to give him a statement of your physical condition, or explain to him your business prosperity. But the child that asks you, "What's that?" "What's it for?" and "What's it made of?" does mean something, and it wants an answer to every question. It wants to know. Could there be a more favorable opportunity of imparting knowledge? How any one can resist such inquiries is a mystery. There is a pleasure in answering children's questions. There is also danger in repressing their curiosity. Every time that the father or mother commands silence when the child asks a question, or puts it off with "Little folks must not know everything," that father or mother does the child an injury by quelling the spirit of inquiry by which it gains most of its knowledge; and if this process be continued for any length of time, the child at last makes no further efforts to acquire knowledge. Instead of quieting the child when it is inclined to ask questions, by putting it off with evasive answers, we should do everything in our power to arouse such a spirit. The plan which too many of us adopt, I am afraid, tends to quell the spirit of inquiry. I have seen men in the professor's chair and on the school platform who, when asked by the pupils any question that did not come directly under the lesson of the day, gruffly silenced them by saying that such questions had nothing to do with the lesson, or evaded answering by remarking that their sphere was not to answer but to put questions. Don't smile, incredulous reader; there are such, and I draw no fancy sketch.

The husbandman, when he finds a piece of ground on which there is nothing growing except here and there a little plant, the seed for which may have been carried there by accident and found a resting-place, and the soil of which is a rich, mellow loam, just in the fittest condition for the reception of the seed of future harvests, does not think of first passing over that land with a roller to pack the soil as tight as possible before he scatters the seed; nor does he, on the other hand, when he finds the soil of his fields baked by the rays of the sun, plant his seed before he first ploughs and harrows that ground and puts it in proper condition. The operations of the judicious teacher or parent are similar. When he finds the child inquisitive, he does n't first stifle the spirit of inquiry, and thus unfit the mind for the reception of knowledge; nor does he, when he finds the pupil dull and inactive, attempt to instil knowledge until he has first aroused the spirit of inquiry, until he has first prepared the soil for the reception of the seed. The processes are mainly similar, except that almost every child is born with this spirit of inquiry in its mind, and is free from any taint until spoiled by either the parent or the teacher, whereas, much of the soil, as it comes into the hands of the husbandman, has, by accident of some kind, already had scattered over it the seeds of weeds now growing in luxuriance.

Every one has noticed with what eagerness and pleasure a child seems to gather knowledge day after day at its home, on the streets, or in the fields and woods. He cares nothing whatever for dry, arbitrary forms. He is a close student of nature, and follows out nature's plan of learning. But this does n't exactly suit us; so we catch the little fellow and lead him to the school-house, and there, with a number of others of the same age, or size, or advancement, we say he goes to school. He seems to think that is more like going to prison, the plan of getting knowledge there is so different from the plan he pursued at home. He no longer studies nature's objects, but sits at a little desk and has a book or a card put before his eyes, on which are twenty-six characters of almost every imaginable shape, and, after being told that these constitute the alphabet, he is asked to study them. How his bright dreams have vanished! This is school-life. Do you wonder that he does n't like it, and that he shouts with delight the moment he gets outside? It is n't because he has had such a pleasant day of it. Quite the contrary. He is glad that he is once more free and permitted to enjoy himself in the open air or at his home. He is free once more to glean knowledge as his inclinations direct him. He finds but little similarity existing between the plan he has been accustomed to pursue and the school plan of acquiring knowledge. Certainly there is a mistake in one plan or the other. In which shall we look for it? We dare not question the wisdom of God, who is the author of this natural method. There is but one ground left for us to take, and it is, that the mistake lies in our plan of teaching.

Many of our primary and ungraded schools are not well conducted. We make them too much the means of acquiring mere book knowledge, and neglect that which the mind of the child directly craves, a knowledge of things. Don't understand me to depreciate the knowledge of words and all that pertains to them. These are of vital importance so far as they convey ideas to the child's mind; but as mere dry forms, distinct from all ideas and thoughts, they are to him worthless. Hence the teacher in our primary school and the parent in the home should follow more closely nature's method and less the method of man, by giving more culture to the perceptive faculties. If you ask me how this can be done, I answer, let your child have more to do with objects when it enters school and less with books. Place in your school-room or in the nursery a number of little shelves or boxes, and in these put all kinds of objects both of nature and of art — pieces of cloth and calico, bits of leather, strings, and patches; samples of wood, minerals, and metals; botanical, geological, and other specimens — anything in which the child would be interested. Let it be an *omnium gatherum*, a general assortment of everything you can collect. If you know anything about object-teaching — and you should — take up one or more of these specimens at a time, and have a general talk about it, either with the school or with the younger members of it. Let them ask all the questions they can, and answer only those which they cannot answer for themselves. Thus you will be following out the natural plan, and the pupils will not only be interested in every lesson, but they will also find it pleasanter to attend school. I don't insist, by any means, that you shall spend the whole time in exercises of this kind, but a short exercise occasionally will soon serve to wake up the minds of your children. The teacher can do more than the parent, because he can have a greater collection of objects, and he has really more time and greater facilities for the preparation necessary to success. It is not any more difficult for the child to learn in this way than it is for it to learn the name of an apple and the names of its different parts and qualities. While it is gleaning knowledge and gathering facts by its own observation, it, at the same time, is gaining a stock of language; for, of course, the judicious teacher will not forget to associate the name with the thing or the quality itself.

Much valuable knowledge, which, probably, you and I lack even yet, might be imparted by means of comparison. As an instance, take a piece of cloth or a piece of calico, and compare its texture and strength with that of other pieces. I have no doubt there are many of my readers who would be as sorely at fault as myself in distinguishing minute differences. All knowledge of the kind, while it would furnish a valuable discipline, would, at the same time, be practical as being useful in after-life. By such training much useful knowledge might be imparted, and children would not fail to be interested. Gaining knowledge in this way would prove a delight to children, and few more effectual means of preventing truancy could be devised.

Spenser says, "Exhaustive observation is an element in all great success." If so — and it does not admit of doubt — it concerns you and me as well as our children or pupils. It is true of the artist; it is true of the physician; it is true of the mechanic; it is true of every calling in life. Yet how many there are of us who wander through the world in a manner blind, or but half awake! One man strolls out among the beauties of nature, and returns, having seen nothing; whereas another will travel over the same route, and return with his blood aglow and his whole frame quivering with excitement. He does n't wait for you to ask him what he has seen, but the moment he has a chance he pours such a volume of description on you that you are puzzled to know where he could have found so much to talk about. What is the difference between Hawthorne and most of our other American writers? He stands above them all in description, not because he was a finer scholar, but because he was a closer observer. The true poet is always a close observer, and it is a part of his education to give the observing faculties special culture. He finds beauty and poetry in waterfalls, forests, and precipices, where the ordinary man sees nothing but mill-sites, lumber-piles, and stone-quarries. The grand or picturesque scene which the young lady dismisses with "Is n't that pretty!" furnishes to him study for an hour or a day, and his poem shows that he has, with the grandeur of the scene, also drawn in the inspiration to picture it in words. The same scene has been presented to both. One has seen nothing in it beyond a pleasant mingling of water, rocks, and trees, while the other has made it a study and has found its real beauty. The success of Bryant and all the other poets of nature is due to the fact that they have trained themselves to be close observers of nature's workings. They see that which escapes your eye and mine; not because their eyes are better or their sight more keen, but because we have not accustomed ourselves to observe as closely as they. Many of us walk daily amid the most beautiful scenery and we know it not. We are surrounded by beauty that would charm the true poet, and yet we are blind. Poor, heedless beings! we enjoy but the half of life. Shall our children be equally unfortunate? Shall they, too, with eyes bent to the earth in search of stray pieces of silver or gold, pass unnoticed the beauties of the heaven above them? Shall we train them like the greyhound, to see nothing but the game ahead? Rather let us train them to look upon nature as a book from which knowledge is to be gleaned in every paragraph, to read the history stored up in the rocky pages in the hearts of her mountains, to examine and study the beauty found in the tiniest leaf or blade of grass, and thus be enabled to lead them from the study of nature to its grand Creator.

A most important part of our education, the culture of the senses, is usually neglected. We do but little toward the training of sight, hearing, and the other senses. We know in our own case that these senses are not so acute as they might be, had they received the proper culture. Do you doubt this? Can you distinguish between the different shades of color, of red, for instance, without having each before you? I know of one man at least with whom all the darker shades of red are maroon. I know of others, too, who are unable to distinguish between the different shades of blue. There are many who know but seven colors instead of the great number of shades. There may be such a thing as color-blindness to account for a part of this defect, but not for the whole of it. The same defect exists in the case of the other senses, in some, probably, to a less, but in others to a greater extent. The blind learn to read by means of raised letters. Their sense of touch becomes so acute that they distinguish objects very readily between which we would be unable to notice any difference except with the eye. It is said, also, that the boys in our blind asylums learn to distinguish their different playmates by hearing them walk. Thus they illustrate in both cases the extent to which the senses may be cultivated. What is done by the blind in the improvement of hearing and touch may be done equally well by those who possess sight. It is altogether a mistaken notion that a man's strength all goes into his left arm when he loses his right, or that his hearing becomes any more acute when he loses the sense of sight. Did he not exercise his left arm more than heretofore, it would be no stronger, and did he not cultivate the sense of hearing more actively, it would be no more acute. So, also, in the case of the deaf and dumb, their sense of sight seems to become much more keen because, being deprived of hearing, they depend much necessarily on the sense of sight. This sense in reality takes the place of both, and it is, therefore, more highly cultivated, and becomes much more active. There is not a single one of the senses that may not be made more acute by judicious use and culture, and the necessity of their culture is too obvious to need argument.

To recapitulate briefly, let me say that I believe it to

be the duty of parents and teachers to arouse in the child a spirit of inquiry. When curiosity manifests itself, gratify it if you can ; if you cannot, don't repress it, and thus stifle it. Give your child every opportunity to study nature. Cultivate its observing faculties even if some of the usual school branches must be omitted. Let the first steps in knowledge be such as are pleasant. Don't prevent a child's becoming acquainted with things. I have thought sometimes that Dr. Wentworth, of Beecher's "Norwood," understood these matters better than most parents, when he preferred that culture for his daughter Rose, which made her acquainted with the secrets of nature. I wish there were many parents of this kind. Our culture would be more effective.

CHAPTER VIII.

MAKING HOMES AND SCHOOLS PLEASANT.

THERE seem to be two distinct classes of persons in all society, those who are striving to make a living and those who are striving to live. Of the former there are too many, of the latter, I am afraid, too few. The care and anxiety incident to many kinds of business often lead men away from all considerations of comfort, and they never learn what pleasure and happiness they might have enjoyed, until it is too late. Poor, deluded mortals! they struggle a whole lifetime making a living, with the hope that they shall some time be able to retire from active business and enjoy the pleasures of life; but to the greater number that time never comes. Now and then one shakes off the dust of the counting-room and creeps out from the heat, and dirt, and noise of the city; and, when the most valuable part of his life is spent, builds himself a rural mansion that a prince might covet, and when he is ready to enjoy it, dies. Others there are in easy circumstances who never know, from the day of their birth to the day of their death, what it is to take a breath of pure air. Do you wonder that their faces are pale? Most of them are striving to make a living, struggling day after day with the world in the doubly vain effort to accumulate wealth, which proves to them, in the end, anything but a blessing.

There are men, too, in the world, who seem scarcely to know that they have homes, making them simply a sort of feeding and sleeping place. There are business men who find it impossible to throw off for a moment the cares of their calling, and enjoy themselves with their families. There are others, too, to whom the billiard saloon or the club-room and corner grocery seem to present greater attractions than the family fireside. I pity the families of such. They are deprived of many of the pleasures of life; but there is usually something wrong somewhere. Is it in the home and its surroundings? or is it in the manner in which the home affairs are managed? There are homes that scarcely deserve the name, there is so little of the home feeling in them; and there are others again, the surroundings of which render them cheerless and unpleasant.

What sort of home have you? I don't want to know how many acres of land you possess, nor whether your house is built of wood, or brick, or stone. I care nothing about all this. Let me look into your house. Are your walls bare and white? Are your carpets kept so studiously from the sunlight and air that they smell musty? Do you keep your parlor closed — as Irving tells us the Dutch do — except when opened for the weekly scrubbing or for a funeral? Do you keep your shutters bolted and your blinds closed lest a stray ray of sunshine should discolor your carpet? Good housewife, if you say yes to all these questions, don't ask why it is that your husband is always away on business or down street, and your children discontented and unhappy. Probably the fault is yours, not theirs. It is n't pleasant to have bare, blank walls to look at. Put some pictures on them. If you can't afford high-priced pictures, get the best you can afford. I believe that every dwelling and every schoolroom in the land should have engravings and pictures on its walls. It will cost something, no doubt; but it is a thousand times better to spend a few dollars in decorating the walls of your dwelling than have your husband spend the same amount at the groggery or even the club-room.

Parents sometimes wonder why it is that their children are discontented and anxiously looking forward to their time for leaving the old homestead. Many youths are anxious to go to the city to seek their fortunes. Why is it? Not because young men and young women from the country succeed better in the city than those "to the manor born," for the temptations which surround every young person in the city are frequently too strong for them to resist, and certain ruin is then the inevitable result. No, this is not the reason. There is often something wrong at home. In many cases, if you were to go with them to their homes, you would find these not only cheerless, but well-nigh forbidding or repulsive. I do not say that it is so in every case; for now and then a young man's ambition leads him to seek a wider field of operation than is presented to him in his own neighborhood, and he goes to some other section or to the city, in which he may expand to his fullest capacity. But it isn't by any means this that sends most away from home. Were their homes made what home should be, they would never think of wandering off. Recall to your mind for a moment the appearance of the homesteads in your own neighborhood, or as many of them, at least, as you have had opportunity to examine, or even notice accurately. How many of them come up to your idea of a pleasant dwelling-place? How many of them would you like to adopt as your place of residence without alteration or addition? The number isn't hard to count, is it? But your neighborhood is no exception to neighborhoods and communities in general. You will find it so everywhere, that too little attention is paid to the decoration and beautifying of homesteads. Every one that has travelled to any extent knows how rare a thing it is to see from the car-window a snug-looking, cosey place; and when such a one does appear, it never fails to attract the attention of the traveller and win his admiration.

What reason can there be for this lack of beauty? Business men tell us they have no time to think of such things; their minds are wholly absorbed in business matters. Reader, will you accept their excuse? I cannot. I care not how pressing business may be, nor how much of a man's time it may occupy, he has no right to neglect those comforts and pleasures that would tend to make his family love and enjoy their home. Man, it seems to me, was not created to be a mere machine, and some of our business men seem to be but little more. If getting money were the chief end to be attained, some of us, I fear, would be found quite far off the track. But we have a higher destiny than this. No man has a right to permit his business so far to engross his time as to rob his family of the social pleasure which is their due. Independent of this, however, there is also a moral question which arises here. The influence of a beautiful home, though the beauty may be simple and unostentatious, in forming the moral character of the young is very great. It is not surprising that many of the lower classes are rough and rude. Much of it may be traced to the appearance of their homes. The skeptical may doubt this, but it is nevertheless true. There is a connection between the beautiful and the good. We seldom find one who has been reared among beautiful scenes, whose childhood has been made happy by a beautiful home, that is rude and uncivil. The little fellow that would n't hesitate a moment to break in the windows of a dingy old house on his way home from school, could not be coaxed to kick to pieces the daisies, and forget-me-nots, and verbenas on his little sister's flower-bed. He has respect for the beautiful. We look for ruffians to come out of such homes as have none of this element of beauty in them. When we see a homestead with broken-down fences, begrimed walls, and filthy, we naturally look for slovenly children to come from that house. Children of this kind flourish in such hovels. We don't expect much good of them, and generally we are not disappointed. We are not much surprised to hear the little fellows swear and use vulgar language, because profanity and vulgarity luxuriate in such soil. It is a fact beyond denial, that the beauty of a home has much to do with the morals of the children reared there. There are exceptions to the rule in such cases where children have been spoiled by indulgence or bad family government; but in general the rule is true.

I know of no surer way to tempt a boy's jack-knife than to place before him rude and ungainly furniture. The furniture of many school-houses is, I am afraid, sometimes a sore temptation to the little urchins in attendance. There are those in which the furniture seems, by its very looks, to say to the boy, "Here's a chance to test the temper and keenness of your blade; try me." And there are those again in which neat, attractive furniture forbids the very idea of its being scratched or cut, and the boys are afraid to attack it, except now and then one of the rudest of the rude. It is unwise economy to put any other than attractive furniture in any schoolroom. A case occurs to me now in which a public hall was to be furnished with benches. The authorities were advised to put in good, neat, substantial furniture, as it was to last. In their wisdom, they saw fit to disregard the advice, and in eight months were compelled to refurnish the same room. They were a second time advised to put in substantial, or, at least, neat, if not substantial benches. Though the same kind of furniture was selected as before, it was given several coats of paint and was grained to imitate maple. This furniture has now been in use several years, and looks almost as well as the day it was put there. No notch, no writing, or anything else of the kind disfigures it, whereas that in use but eight months was covered with pencil-marks and scratches. It pays, and that seems to be a consideration, to provide neat and durable furniture for school-rooms. I might prove this by a great number of incidents that have fallen under my own observation, but it is unnecessary. What is true in the case of school furniture is also true elsewhere. Neat furniture is not necessarily expensive. There are those, I know, who would object to purchasing expensive furniture; hence I meet this objection. Every one knows that in the home, too, children are much more careful of that furniture which is pretty than of that which contains none of the elements of beauty.

How shall we make our homes pleasant? The question has been partly answered in what has been said before. I give no advice here as to the color of your walls. They may be white or some neutral tint, but don't let them be bare as if hewn out of solid rock. Have some pictures or engravings with which to decorate them, however small these may be. Be careful, however, what pictures you place there; for each one of them will, day after day, stamp itself deeper and deeper on the minds of your children who see it. Remember you are not placing them there for the purpose of winning the passing applause or admiration of your visitors, but for the purpose of making your home an enchanting place for your own family as well as for strangers. Let, therefore, nothing but the purest sentiments of the heart be taught by your pictures. The same remark will apply to the school-room, that dreary and forbidding place that it so often is. Adorn its walls with engravings, cards, and pictures. They will cheer it up, and be a sort of verification of the poet's idea of making

"The desert blossom as the rose."

Drive out that cold and cheerless feeling which causes children often to feel that the school-room is the unpleasantest place on earth. You can do this partly by decorating your walls with pictures and engravings. Don't let the blank walls stare your pupils in the face any longer. There is something almost ghostly in them; they are, at least, cheerless.

School-houses and homes may be made pleasant by beautifying them with flowers and shrubbery. Most persons know that it will improve the appearance of their homes to plant shrubbery on their grounds, and thus they make them attractive to strangers; but there are few who plant because of the moral effect it may have on their children. Flowers have a humanizing influence. One feels greater safety when he falls into the hands of those fond of flowers and the cultivation of them. We are all fond of them, but we sadly neglect cultivating them, sometimes on account of the expense or the trouble it may cost us. The natural love for flowers is so great that little need be said on this point to parents, and yet it is true, too, that many might make their homes much more pleasant, especially in the winter, if more care were taken to cultivate flowers. The care of a single pot of plants in the window, it has been said, may serve to change the current of a man's whole lifetime. Add to this the influence it has in softening the manners and humanizing the feelings of a family, and the care of flowers becomes an invaluable pastime. There are few who cannot find space for at least a few pots of plants or flowers.

How is it in our school-rooms? In how many of them, even in summer, the most propitious season, do we find flowers growing in the yards surrounding the house? True, there are many which do not even have an enclosure, and the school grounds extend indefinitely. I am partial to extensive school grounds, but I don't like to have them as extensive and as boundless as the highways along which they stretch. In a house surrounded by such grounds one feels much as he would on a ship in mid-ocean or in a hut in the desert. No limits are in sight. But, seriously, it is an evil that so many of our school-houses are located in such inaccessible, unhealthy, and unpleasant places. Miasmatic swamps and bleak or rocky hillsides are not the best places, though they may be the cheapest. Of all places, the school-house should occupy the pleasantest and most healthy. It is time that public sentiment break down the mistaken and unwise economy of directors and school commissioners in purchasing for building sites such land as can be bought for the smallest amount of money, but which is wholly unfit for the erection of any building. The welfare and health of our children demand something better than the waste land in the angle of some cross-roads or the brier-patch of some hillside. But to say nothing further of the unfortunate location of many buildings in respect to healthfulness, many are not favorably located with regard to beautifying them and making their grounds attractive and pleasant for the teacher and the pupils. I have in my mind now school-houses literally "founded upon a rock" and built amidst rocks, the interior furnished with one long desk running around three sides of the room, with slabs for benches. It would be well-nigh impossible to render these attractive and homelike. But this is the dark side of the picture, and such school buildings are happily fast giving way to better ones. The number reported "unfit for use" is rapidly growing less, and we may yet succeed in having none but suitable buildings used for school purposes.

How shall we beautify our school grounds? If they are not already enclosed, it will be necessary to enclose them; for however rigid our laws regarding estrays, we cannot expect to make improvements on open land that will not be interfered with and marred by wandering cattle of some kind. If there is not pride enough in the directors to do their duty, the teacher will in many instances be able, with the help of his pupils and patrons, to enclose a sufficient portion of ground at but little expense. Much of the manual labor necessary will be performed cheerfully by some of the larger boys, and by some scheme of collecting, such as a mite fund or an occasional exhibition, all the necessary money for the purchase of materials can be readily secured. A little labor and some perseverance are necessary.

I recall to mind now the "Old Sandstone," as we endearingly named our school-house. It was built of a formation more modern than Hugh Miller's *old red* sandstone. Its tint was a soft yellowish gray, and its texture coarse. How we boys loved to sit on the old rocks, and, with rounded boulders, wear grooves into them while we imitated, as we thought, a flouring-mill, the clean, gritty, golden sand running down from under our little hands! One spring day the teacher proposed to us that we should enclose a small portion of our grounds for the purpose of planting shrubbery and flowers. Each one contributed something, and all offered their assistance in completing the work. In a short time the necessary funds were collected, and in the course of two weeks our house was surrounded by a neat and durable lattice fence. Though one of the oldest and least attractive in architecture, our school-house became the pride of the township, and it was not without the bitter complaints of its patrons, that years afterward it was thrown down to make place for a new one, and our shrubbery and flower-borders that had cost us so much toil, and which were a source of so much pride, were destroyed by some heartless wretches who seemed to have no sympathy with the beautiful in either art or nature.

Supposing the school grounds enclosed, or, at least that part of them immediately surrounding the house, we are prepared to do something more. If the proper spirit has been engendered in the pupils, there will be no difficulty in securing their assistance in beautifying the grounds. My own experience will bear me out in making this assertion. I have never applied to my pupils for such assistance in vain; and I have asked for it frequently. The teacher has little idea of how much may be accomplished with their assistance, until the work is completed. I confess I have often been surprised at the alacrity with which they enter into any project of the kind. Place confidence in them, and show them that you are in earnest about the matter, and success is certain. It is not my purpose here to give definite rules for laying out the grounds, as that is the province of the landscape gardener. It is taken for granted that every one possesses a sufficient degree of taste to improve the school ground sufficiently, at least, to make it home-like and pleasant; and that is, after all, the purpose of decoration in this case. You can do much by requesting your pupils to bring shrubbery and plants from home. Let them gather spare lilac and rose bushes, cuttings of geraniums and verbenas, mock-orange, spirea, and other low shrubbery, together with such bulbs and seeds as may be gathered in every flower-garden; and you will be surprised at both the variety and the quantity brought to the school-house door. A half-holiday excursion to the woods for cedars, hemlock, spruce, and maples, together with other evergreen and deciduous trees for planting in the grounds, will add materially to the stock, and, with a little care in the setting and culture, you will soon have school grounds which will gladden the hearts not only of you and your pupils, but of all those who look upon your work.

I have never succeeded so well in cheering up my recitation-room in winter as when I placed a few pots of blooming plants on my recitation table or at the window, when not too cold. It costs care and attention, but the good effect it has in brightening up the faces of your pupils and attracting them to your instructions is an ample reward. When cheered up in this way, or even with bouquets of cut flowers, all the gloom that sometimes hangs around a school-room is dispelled and driven off, and a sort of cheeriness, which brightens up the mind, takes its place. Try it, teachers, especially in summer, when there is no danger of the frost-king cutting down the beauty of your pets, and notice the effect produced. Don't stop to argue the trouble of it. If you are heartily engaged in the work you have undertaken, you will think little of the trouble; for certainly if you have entered the profession with the idea of gaining a fortune, or thinking that you will be relieved of anxiety and trouble, you have made a serious mistake in the selection of your calling.

All that has been said in this chapter with regard to making the school-room pleasant and attractive, will apply to the home also. Don't fail to make your home a charming place, one that your children will leave with sadness and regret. When you come to add to its pleasures, don't put everything that is beautiful in your parlor and nothing in your living-room. Remember that it is infinitely more important that you originate these pleasures for the moral influence they may exert over your children than for the gratification they may give your visitors. Among suitable pictures with which to adorn the walls of your living-room none are more appropriate than family portraits To these may be added such others as convey a feeling of cheerfulness and content, such as fruit, flower, and bird pieces, all of which have connected with them agreeable and pleasant associations. Your children will be either contented and happy at home or they will be discontented and restless; and, if your family government is all that it should be, very much will depend upon whether your home and home-life are cheerful, pleasant, and attractive, or otherwise.

CHAPTER IX.

PLAY LIFE.

RICHTER says, "Play is, in the first place, the working off at once of the overflow of both mental and physical powers." There is in every one a fund of play-life. There are, probably, few of us who have wholly forgotten the joyousness of youth and the plays with which we were wont to while away the time. Few there are, too, who do not remember the pleasure they experienced when the animal life and activity which suffused and animated their whole being were no longer smothered and repressed — when they were permitted to expend this activity, this play-life of their being, in that manner which was in most perfect harmony with their feelings. We look back upon those days as among the pleasantest of life.

Reader, have you ever noticed the young of the animal creation? Watch, some bright day in spring, the lambkins as they race with each other around the barn-yard. Notice the feathered tribe, too, as soon as the fledglings are strong enough to leave the nest. An uncontrollable desire seems to urge them to try the strength of their limbs, and, one by one, they hop from branch to branch, until at length their courage strengthens them for longer flights. Have you ever stopped to inquire why these little lambs frisk and gambol around in this lively way? or why the little birds hop from branch to branch when they seem to have no definite purpose? Neither bird nor lamb knows why it does this. God has implanted this activity in them, and they could not keep quiet if they would. They must play; they can't help it. It is a merciful decree of Providence that this activity must be expended in order that the muscles of both may be strengthened and the sinews toughened. What is true in this particular case, is true in the whole animal creation, man included.

Dr. Bushnell remarks on this point, "Having set the young of all the animal races a playing, and made their beginning an age of frisking life and joyous gambol, it would be singular if God had made the young of humanity an exception; or if, having put the same sportive instinct in their nature, he should restrict them always to a carefully practical and sober mood." It would, indeed, be strange if he should deny the young of our own race that happiness, if it can so be called, which he confers upon the young of the inferior portion of the animal kingdom. But he has beneficently implanted the same instinct in our nature, though we may not understand his design in doing so. The little child has this same instinctive love of play that we find in the lamb or the kid. True, we forget God's object in placing it there; but we have no right to question the motive. Every day it manifests itself in some shape. Now it is expended in clambering upon board-piles or climbing up trees, and now again in sundry evolutions and contortions, and all for the fun of it. The movements are well-nigh as capricious as those of the kid or the lamb. We can't explain them, nor do we know what to expect next. The life and activity are there, and no one can predict how they will be manifested. God has placed this life in the child, and it plays because it can't help it, just as one of the lower animals plays when moved by the instinct within. In both it serves the purpose of exercise, and strengthens and develops the body. Notice the boy turning his somersaults in the straw-mow or dancing on the seedy floor, or the girl as she jumps the rope or skips along the pavement, and see if you cannot trace the working of an inner influence which urges on each to play.

This play-life is not found in the child alone, and it were a great mistake to limit it to the young of our race. You and I play in accordance with the designs of Providence, or we fail to fulfil a part of our duty. We look forward to the time that we shall be able to enjoy ourselves more than we do now, to the time, it may be, when we shall be able to retire from active business, and enter upon our real play-life. The lawyer works at his briefs and studies up his cases not because he likes the work, but because he is anxious to accumulate such an amount of money as will place him beyond the reach of want, that he may enter, at some future day, upon his period of play-life. The same is true with every other professional man. The mechanic, too, toils at his bench or in his shop, the merchant in the counting-room, the clerk behind the counter, the farmer in his fields — and all because in the future they see a time when they shall have so far escaped from toil as to be able to rest from their labor and enter upon their time of play. Yet how very few there are who really ever do reap the harvests to which they look forward so eagerly. They repress the desire for play and amusement which they find ever urging them on to activity, vainly hoping that in the future they shall be able to enter upon a period of continual enjoyment. It may be said with truth that those who enjoy life are comparatively few. The period of enjoyment, instead of extending through one's whole life, is postponed until such a time as the cares and anxiety of business no longer interfere, and thus much of life, instead of being a pleasure, is made a burden.

If I interpret the design of Providence correctly in implanting this spirit of play in us, it must be evident to every one that it is wrong to repress it in any way. We have the right to direct it into the proper channels, but no attempt to repress it will be successful. We may build obstructions across the merry brook that ripples over the pebbles at the foot of our garden, but however high we may build to intercept its progress, it is but for a time. When we least expect it, the latent power, whose force we had forgotten to calculate, or a sudden freshet, bursts away the barriers, and deluges and destroys the beauty of our garden; and the greater the opposition to its progress, the greater the strength accumulated to prosecute the work of destruction. Had we placed only such obstructions as were necessary to utilize the power of the brook, no danger would have arisen and no mischief ensued. The same may be said in the life of the child. We may place such obstacles in its way as will silence its merriment and prevent its play and enjoyment, but we do not know what latent power we may be developing. We know not what injury we may be doing the child, or into what evil channel we may be turning the current of life. We are directing the course of a stream whose power we fail to estimate; and there are those of us who attempt not only to check its progress, but, in addition, reverse its course. Forgetful of the natural laws which control the child's actions, we commit the great blunder of trying to resist nature. As well might we, in the case of the stream, attempt to resist the law of gravitation, and try to send its waters up hill. One effort would be no greater failure than the other.

God loves little children too much to place such instincts in their nature as would make them unhappy; and it is, therefore, a great mistake to suppose that play or amusement is in any way opposed to piety. There are those, I know, who would insist on children's being sober-faced and unnatural. I believe play to be the forerunner of religion, in fact, as has been said by another, "the symbol of true Christian liberty;" and, therefore, I can see no reason for attempting to curb or silence the joyousness of child-life, on moral grounds. Morality and mirth are not at enmity. I confess that no man, be he minister or layman, impresses me more favorably with the cause of religion by his being morose or ascetic. I do not believe it necessary for a man to be anything else than natural in order to be religious. I have no faith in that church dogma which requires one to wear the proverbial "parson face." If you feel more solemn on becoming pious, I have no right, of course, to criticize your manifestation of that feeling; and if, on the other hand, the hope of unbounded bliss and happiness in the future life leads me to be more joyous and cheerful, you have no right to question the propriety of my outward life. Your temperament and mine may differ, and our outward conduct will also differ. What is true in your case and mine is true also in the case of the child. He may be pious and inclined at all times to do right, and yet be very cheerful. Instead, therefore, of supposing that behind this play the devil is urging it in order to break down the kingdom of Christ, let us look at the matter soberly, and we shall find that it is but one of the fundamental principles of piety that is being developed.

There are few questions which to honest Christian parents and teachers are of so much concern, and which have given them more anxiety, than that of knowing how to preserve order in school or the family without losing the respect of the children, or, at least, making home or school unpleasant. From the one extreme, of allowing the child to do as it pleases, to the other, of requiring a death-like silence, there are advocates of every grade of discipline. I would, by no means, sanction the government of those who permit their children to do as they please; nor could I, by any means, indorse the course of those who are so rigidly disciplinary that they allow their children no privileges. The middle ground here, as everywhere, is the safest. I have known parents who looked upon a game of ball among young men or boys as almost criminal waste of time, saying, that had they the control of things those same boys should be put into a clover-field to pick stones, thereby getting the same or an equivalent amount of exercise while doing something useful. Such ideas are not only basely utilitarian, but in direct opposition to the design of God. I sometimes fear that we are apt to forget that we were once boys with all the foolish pranks of boys, as we now regard them. We forget that it is just as natural for a boy to be boyish or a child childish as it is for us to be otherwise, and that our enjoyments are to us just what the child's enjoyments are to it. We censure children for being childish, or, in other words, for being themselves, and the result is that in many cases we spoil them, and make them believe themselves men and women.

It is n't pleasant to have noisy children about you, I know; but it is better to have noisy children than to have premature men and women, stiff and starchy as if just prepared to receive a fashionable call. There are those who silence every outburst of glee, as if it were detrimental to the best interests of the family to allow children to be noisy. I believe this to be wrong. I believe that if children find fun or amusement in anything, they should be permitted to enjoy it when such fun or amusement is legitimate. If it grate harshly on our nerves, it is our duty to let them have it in some other part of the house where it will not disturb us; but we have no right, if desirous of their welfare, to stop them unless they are doing some one an injury.

I can imagine no sadder spectacle than a child dragging itself through the world without any enjoyment. Richter draws the apt comparison between it and a butterfly with its four wings torn off and creeping like a worm; and how true this comparison is! A child shorn of all that which would permit it to enjoy life, and made to creep through the world day after day instead of gambolling and frisking through it as instinct and impulse dictate, is in a but little more unfortunate condition than the butterfly deprived of the wings which were to carry it from flower to flower and from one beauty to another, making its life one gay round of pleasure; and the parent or the teacher who robs the child of its pleasure is no less guilty than the rude and wicked school-boy who would tear from the insect its wings. The lives of both victims are made burdensome, but the parent we praise for rearing quiet and sedate children, while the boy we characterize as wicked. Which does God look on with most favor?

We make a great mistake when we are distant or reserved in the presence of our children. We should enjoy life with them. Ruling them at a distance is not without its effect; but, unfortunately, the effect is most disastrous to that blossoming love in the child's bosom which is ready to spring forth into life and beauty, but which is blighted by this chilling frost and never permitted to bloom in perfection. It is rare that he who rules his family with a rod of despotism lives to have his children thank and bless him for his family government. The parent or the teacher who feels it beneath his dignity to unbend at times in the presence of his children or pupils, loses much of his power, and is certainly an object of pity. We must have sympathy with children, that we may exercise a healthful influence over them, and no man should have the government of children unless he can lend this sympathy.

I have known persons who thought themselves disgraced when found playing with children, and I have heard men stigmatized as "old fools" when, for their own and others' amusement, they entered into a game of ball with those ten or twenty years younger than themselves. I liked them all the better for thus relaxing their dignity and making others happy while enjoying themselves, and bringing once more the rose to its old place in the cheek. I like old men with young hearts. They grow old beautifully and are a source of pleasure to every one around them, and when they come to leave us we feel that we are losing something, and their death leaves a wound in our hearts and a void in our circle that keep their memory as green as the sod that covers their graves.

I like men that can make youth and children happy by throwing away dignity and enjoying play with the young. It isn't dignified, possibly, according to the fashionable idea of dignity, to find yourself on the carpet with your little folks tumbling back and forth on top of you, or trying to pull you along the floor, but it certainly does not make a worse man of you for thus indulging in the childish mirth. Dr. Chalmers, it is said, found his greatest fun in playing with boys at rolling stones downhill. Dr. Beecher, too, it is said, loved dearly to romp with his children, and they all thought the more of him for it. Washington Irving, bachelor as he was, says he never felt more respect for Jeffrey, the Scotch jurist and critic, than when he found him in the family of one of his Edinburgh friends playing a romping game with the children. No man is any the worse for thus making childhood happy and renewing memories of his own youth in the sport and play which he shares with the child. We like such men, for they dispense joy as blessings all around them. Children obey such parents more cheerfully, and when the parent relaxes his dignity, and forgets his years for the time, the child reaps the highest enjoyment and loves this play with a love unequalled.

There is no danger whatever that the authority of the parent will be lost. The closer he brings himself into sympathy with the child in his plays, the stronger is the authority made and the more cheerful the obedience of the child. This has been verified in the experience of those who enter into most hearty sympathy with child-life. It is a mistake that a teacher or a parent loses command of children by engaging in play with them. Those parents whose family government is most successful are those who enter into most hearty sympathy with their children, who joy with their joys and sorrow with their sorrows. I know that the old saw, "Familiarity breeds contempt," is quoted again and again to prove that teachers should not engage in the sports of their children. It is n't true. Familiarity with your pupils will not breed contempt unless there is that in you which is contemptible. If you are afraid that in play with them you may display some weakness which you would not have them know, it were better for you to refrain, and if it be any habit that you have reason to be ashamed of, do one of two things, break it up or leave the profession.

How often have we almost envied the pleasures of our boys in winter as they dart past us down the hills with the swiftness of an arrow on their steel-bound sleds and jumpers! How we long to be with them, and yet we dare not! This unnatural dignity which stiffens so many of us prevents us indulging our desire to coast with them. We fear that people would talk about us and call us boyish. When we travel through the northern part of continental Europe we find it royal fun to mount behind a Russian and dart down a hill with such speed as almost drives the breath from our bodies. Yet this is the same sport in which our boys alone engage. There is n't any difference, and there is no reason whatever why you and I should not join them. There is no doubt that we would enjoy it; the very sparkle in our eyes, as we stand watching the young folks, tells as plainly as it can be told that our hearts are with them.

Of late, skating, a charming sport and healthful recreation, has admitted to its enjoyments both sexes. Few place a full estimate on the good that has been done by the establishment of skating parks and rinks in our cities and larger towns within the past few years. It has brought back to the cheek of many a young lady the rose

whose place had been usurped by the lily. It has furnished, while contributing greatly to health, both pleasure and excitement, and thus has insured for itself a popularity not easily shaken. It has admitted to its pleasures all ranks and conditions of whatever age and sex, and while the rinks and parks in the cities have popularized the amusement there, they have also served to awaken a new interest in the exercise in the country, and now it has become a rare thing to find a youth living along a stream of any considerable size who is unable to skate. Thus while it has, by its popularity, become fashionable and interesting, it has at the same time, been conducive to health, and been the means of doing much good.

In general it may be said that we have too little amusement in common with our children. Had we more fun and amusement with them, and did we join more in their plays, it is likely that we should need fewer billiard-rooms, fewer balls, fewer horse-races, and other questionable amusements. Did we indulge more in the harmless sports of youth, while we would inculcate in our children a love for the pleasures of home-life, we would feel less like giving questionable and illegitimate amusements our encouragement and sanction by keeping silent with regard to their vicious results. The rising generation and our own would both be the better for it. We would have less vice, less immorality, and enjoy life the more.

Don't think that I would make the whole of child-life play-life. There are restrictions now and then to be

placed on its plays. When work is to be performed, the play must for the time be put aside. Duty must always moderate the amount of play. The child will soon understand that restrictions will be encountered in the home, in the school, and in the church, as often as one or another of these demands such restrictions. But if the child be trained properly, duty will never be looked upon as hostile to play. He will soon feel that obedience to both play-life and duty will serve to give him that symmetrical development which he needs.

Care must be taken that the child be permitted to engage in those plays only which are entirely free from vicious tendencies. Those plays which would do injury to another or to any of God's creatures are essentially wrong, and the child must not be allowed to engage in them. A play that would tend to mar the beauty with which God has surrounded us, such as throwing at any beautiful object in nature, should not be permitted. Stoning birds, playing tricks on one another, with many other sports of a similar nature, not only are not beneficial, but are in themselves calculated to do harm, and hence the child should be prevented from engaging in them. The same might be said of those which have a tendency to lead to the formation of bad habits, such as playing marbles for gain, which is but a form of gambling, say the best of it. There are so many plays in which the child may indulge which are not objectionable, that we should give no countenance to any that may have an immoral tendency.

If possible, this restless activity, which many parents

suppose to be latent mischief, should be expended in the open air. Nature's machinery is so admirably adapted to the wants to be supplied, that the store of fresh and pure air is inexhaustible ; hence out-door sports will be found much the most invigorating to both body and mind. There are times, however, when preparation must also be made to entertain children in the house, unless we permit them to take care of themselves on the streets during the evening, a most reprehensible practice which we find in vogue often in cities and in larger villages. Here is where the mother will find room to exercise unlimited skill and judgment in making her home-life so pleasant as to present greater attractions to her children than any other spot on earth, and the true Christian mother will find it her greatest pleasure to minister to the comfort and cheerfulness of her little children.

CHAPTER X.

PASTIMES AND AMUSEMENTS.

I ENTER here upon the discussion of a topic which presents in some of its parts unusual difficulties, from the fact that upon some points there is an unparalleled diversity of opinion. It is a matter of some importance to both teacher and parent to know in what pastimes or amusements children should engage. In general, it may be said, a close inspection is necessary, that children may indulge in those plays only which tend to elevate and create a proper sentiment, and that those should be discarded which may in any way have an evil tendency.

It is as natural for the child to play with its toys, as it is for the adult to be interested in such tools as he may have daily occasion to handle. Every child should have a supply of playthings. It is not necessary that this supply should be either extensive or costly. The doll which the little girl carries so carefully, possesses almost as much real interest for the child, as the babe in its mother's arms does for her; and no jockey or turfman is prouder of his steed, than is the little boy with his broom-stick or hoe-handle as he capers and prances through the yard. Who shall say that the little girl's "pieces of chaney," as she calls them, are not a source of as much pleasure as is her mother's gilt China set to her? Who can tell the wealth of the odds and ends of things, the buttons, marbles, scraps of leather, pieces of painted glass, bits of tin, horse-chestnuts, top, slate-pencils, sticks, and blocks which one finds on emptying a little urchin's pocket? Do we call them trash? They are a source of endless pleasure to him, and were his pocket thrice as large, he would have thrice the variety to fill it. He is not bothered with bank-notes and railway or government bonds. A few nickel cents in the corner of his pocket to spend now and then for candy is all the riches he cares for if he is permitted to enjoy himself in his own way.

It is not necessary to furnish children with a great quantity of expensive toys with which to amuse themselves. I have known a child to put aside the prettiest of dolls to carry around in its arms an old slipper or a boot, and it seemed to derive as much pleasure from this as from the other. Who shall say that the little daughter of poverty is not as much pleased with her rag-doll, with ink-spots for eyes, as is the dainty little pet of luxury with her ten-dollar wax-doll, with curls, and eyes that seem to close when it is put to sleep? The principle is true also in the case of other toys and playthings. Give children an opportunity to gather some playthings for themselves, and supply them with a few others such as their tastes seem to prefer, and you will have done much toward enabling them to enjoy themselves.

Picture-books form a source of great amusement to the child. When in the power of the parent, it should be furnished with these. Every one has noticed how eagerly the child opens every new book it lays hold of, to see the pictures, and should nothing but bare words meet the eye, the book is soon put aside; but should it contain engravings or pictures, it amuses itself for hours in examining them, if they are such as please it. I doubt the policy, however, of placing in the hands of the child such pictures as it cannot understand, or those familiarly known as fairy-pictures. We can accomplish much greater good by giving the child a book containing pictures of such objects as surround it. It will be remembered here that I speak especially of small children. They take but little interest in those pictures which they do not comprehend, and if left to their own choice, they will select such as they are acquainted with

There is in every child an imitative faculty. When you read, as if to satirize you, it picks up a book, and when a stranger drops in, or while you sit in your easy chair, it makes its little self comfortable, and, with eyes bent closely on the book open before it, imitates you, innocently supposing that it is doing the same work that you are doing. The little girl, seeing her mother sew; is anxious to engage in the same employment, and feels herself particularly happy when she is allowed the use of a needle and thread and is given a few patches to sew together. The boy, too, anxious to be engaged in the same work as the man, and being endowed with a constructive instinct — if we can call it such — lays hold of the first tools he can and becomes a mock carpenter. Reader, did you never, when a boy, on a cold winter's night, when the snow and the storm without made you feel glad to remain in the house, sit beside the kitchen fire and build yourself an imaginary house or church of corncobs? I think I can yet see myself with my playfellows sitting, when a boy, by the blazing wood-fire, and planning my imaginary houses and erecting them of these same rude materials. I was not the fortunate possessor of a set of building-blocks, so my resort was corncobs, and how I enjoyed them! You may smile, but I doubt if ever a son of luxury is more content than the farmer-boy with his little house constructed with his own hands. I would have a set of blocks, building-blocks, if attainable, in the hands of every child. If building-blocks could not be readily secured, or if thought too expensive, any blocks that would enable the child to build houses, walls, or fences, would answer. Permit little girls to do all the sewing they wish. They may lose a needle now and then, but that is a matter of small moment compared with the amount of good accomplished.

Children are fond of studying nature and holding converse with her. They delight to ramble in the woods and through the meadows in search of berries and wild flowers. They delight in wandering along the gravelly beds of the meandering brooks in search of shells and pebbles. They take an interest in those things which, from their apparent insignificance, escape the attention of the adult. They find pleasure and amusement in that which we are accustomed to pass by unnoticed. To them, as to the painter or the naturalist, every blade of grass or clump of moss, every shining shell or pearly pebble possesses a peculiar beauty and interest unknown to the careless observer. All this argues the necessity of granting them enjoyment of this kind. Often the disposition of teachers and parents is to curb this spirit in the child. They look upon it as the beginning of a vagabond sort of life, and sagely predict an indolent future, forgetting that this very life which the child is inclined to lead requires tenfold more labor and exertion than any task which they would assign it. So the little fellow is debarred the privilege and pleasure of rambling among the objects of nature, and is required to remain within the circumscribed limits of the enclosure which surrounds his home. I would, by no means, have the child unrestricted in its rambles. I think there is danger, in such a case, that it may become restive under restraint in time, if permitted too free a range. As a source of amusement and enjoyment, however, the child should now and then be permitted to roam at will. In addition to the enjoyment which it may derive, it also gleans much useful information, and cultivates its faculties for observation, and thus strengthens powers which, in the future, may put to blush the knowledge of many a young man who with egotistic pride flaunts his diploma in the face of the public.

Occasional excursions of the whole school may add much to the enjoyment of the children, and they will at the same time do much toward strengthening and developing the physical system, and thus be promotive of health. These excursions are also beneficial as recreation from too close, and sometimes too tedious, attention to books and study. We pay too little attention in our system of education to learning the secrets of nature. Ofttimes more can be learned in the study of botany from an hour's excursion over the meadows or through the woods than could be gleaned from a dozen recitations in the school-room; and the same is true in other branches of natural science. I like the old-fashioned nuttings that we used to take when I was a school-boy. Now and then we used to be chased by sundry dogs and frightened by sundry men, and it was terribly hard on boots and breeches; but we enjoyed it, and the exercise we had was both healthful and pleasant. Children should be encouraged to go on these excursions oftener than they do. Of course, it is to be expected that some one in the neighborhood of the school will grumble against it; but then if the excursion is made outside of school hours, it is a matter that does not concern any one specially but yourself and the children. Parents, too, should join in these parties, and enjoy themselves with their children.

The growing tendency in our busy age is to pay too little attention to birthdays and holidays. These return so seldom that there is no reason whatever why we should not enjoy them with our children when they do come. I am not of those who believe that a child's life should be one continuous season of festivity and gayety; but I do believe in occasional enjoyment of this kind. No one could appreciate these festivities if they occurred daily. As Richter says, "Not even a grown-up head could stand being crowned every day by a new country." But this objection cannot be urged against birthdays and the usual holidays. Memory carries us back to the time when the day before Christmas the teacher used to send two boys to his home, who returned laden with baskets of candies and cakes, which were distributed among us as a sort of bribe against barring him out; and it always had its due effect. We felt as grateful for our sweetmeats and as proud of them, as we now do over the finest volume of Shakspeare as a Christmas present; and yet this was only an earnest of the day to come, when jellies, and cakes, and pies, and puddings, and the usual turkey, were placed before us. So, too, on the annual return of the birthday of some one of the family, we feasted and made merry. The nicest of cake, confectionery, and fruit tempted the palate, and the family reunion was among the pleasantest occurrences of the year. What utilitarianism shall say that it was all a waste of time and a subjection to the animal appetites? Little does the utilitarian dream of the amount of enjoyment clustering in one of these family festive occasions, when business and all harassing cares are, for the moment, shut out, and the social powers given full play.

Children, as well as adults, need the society of one another. Don't think that it is a lack of love for you that sends them scampering to their fellows when an opportunity occurs. Could you adapt yourself to the companionship of these little folks, they would seek your company just as eagerly as they now seem to seek that of other children. They are endowed with the same social instincts that we possess, and, unless we silence these, they will seek companions. An important duty devolves here upon the parent and upon his representative, the teacher, in the selection of fit companions for the child. Shall a child which has contracted no bad habits and which knows no evil, be allowed to associate with all kinds of playmates? or shall it be limited to those which are known to be as pure as itself? There seems to be no middle ground here. A false argument may be urged that its influence on the spoiled child may be good, and that it, therefore, should be allowed to associate with all sorts of companions. The result in this case would be much the same as that produced by putting a balky horse and a young colt in the same team — a short time will suffice to make the beginner as vicious as the one already hardened. A question urges itself upon our attention here. Should children's parties be encouraged? My reply to this would be: on certain conditions, certainly. If children at children's parties will be children, and enjoy themselves as such, these parties will be promotive of much good, and they should be encouraged; but if the tendency is to make them feel that they are already little men and women, and that they should conduct themselves as such, then they are harmful, and the parent who tolerates them is not wise. I know of nothing more pleasant to a child than to allow it, on its birthday or some similar occasion, to invite a number of its associates and friends to join it for the afternoon. I have, however, known little parties of this kind which, it seemed to me, were held at unseasonable hours — from seven to ten or eleven at night. I think such a course unwise in parents. The child's health will be endangered soon enough without depriving it of some of its most precious hours of sleep. Nor should these parties be held too often. Much of their virtue consists in their novelty. This same remark may be applied to all amusements of the child. There should not be too frequent a repetition of them. The appetite becomes sated, as the children of the affluent, who have everything they desire, can testify.

School celebrations, concerts, or exhibitions, are often valuable as amusements. They serve also, in addition to amusement, to arouse interest. Many a boy looks forward with eagerness, like many an older boy, to the day when he shall mount the rostrum to make his celebration or exhibition speech. He knows very well that father and mother and his sisters will be there to hear him, and he looks for their approbation, just as the orator looks for the smiles and applause of his audience, or the young bachelor for the approving smile and bouquet of some one that he knows is in the audience, as he rises to deliver his graduating oration. It does them each good to receive this praise, and who could have the courage to deny them?

Lastly, as a pastime and source of enjoyment, I refer to music, and especially music on that most perfect of musical instruments, the human voice. If there is one thing above others that would prove acceptable to God, it seems to me it must be praise in psalms and hymns of thanksgiving. How it thrills one's heart to hear the happy voices of children in beautiful concord "singing for Jesus glad hymns of devotion"! It seems to me no one can remain unmoved as a band of little children, pure and such as Christ would have us to be, stand with upturned faces and uplifted voices singing to the Saviour. Reader, did it ever strike you, when listening to these happy songs, that Jesus may be standing by your side listening with you? How solemn and yet how beautiful the thought!

CHAPTER XI.

THE INFLUENCE OF HOME EXAMPLE.

AS I have watched a child, when engaged in play, imitating all the processes and occupations of those by whom it is surrounded, I have thought how easily we can tell the way in which a household is managed by watching the habits which the child has contracted, and how necessary it is that the parent should be careful to engage in nothing which he does not wish the shrewd observer of human nature to detect. I would not set this up as an unerring test, but in the great majority of cases, one is able, by a close observance of the manner in which children conduct themselves, to tell much of what home-life is like. It is a rare thing that a child possesses so much individuality that the home life and home manners do not, to a great extent, modify its conduct. Now and then, it is true, we meet with one on whom home associations seem to have no influence; but rarely. As I have watched one of my own little ones, and seen myself burlesqued so perfectly that for the moment I was almost driven to the conclusion that I was being ridiculed, I have felt that one cannot be too careful in making his life exemplary.

If we take the trouble to bring up before us our home life and manner that we may examine it thoroughly,

I am afraid there are few of us who would be willing to overlook in others' what we expect to have overlooked in our own. Daily indiscretions come up so rapidly before us in review that we are glad to bury the past, and make retribution, at least so far as promises go, in the good deeds of the future. There is no doubt that there is room for improvement in my case and yours as well as in our neighbor's. Don't let us turn to the consideration of his case until we have first satisfactorily disposed of our own.

Few parents appear to know how readily their own habits can be traced by the care they take of the children. When we look over a school-room full of children, we wonder sometimes why it is that, while here and there are some whose dress is clean and hair smoothed, there are so many others whose appearance is widely different from the former. We can judge nothing of the pecuniary condition of the families from which these different classes of children come. They are but the exponent of the home-life, and we are not disappointed, when we follow the little fellow with greasy hands and clothes and unkempt hair to his home, to find that his mother and her house are not by any means patterns of cleanliness. There are nameless little inconveniences arising from the want of cleanliness which one would think are sufficient to drive mothers to a better care of their children: but not so. They will allow them to appear in public, and they send them abroad sometimes in a condition anything but pleasant to a cleanly person.

The teacher frequently can do much to improve the child's condition in this particular. A kindly request that all will appear in the school-room with hair neatly combed, clothes and shoes brushed, and face and hands washed clean, with now and then the proper amount of praise for any visible improvement in these matters, rarely fails to produce the desired result. I take it for granted that at this late day no teacher can be found whose own appearance in these respects is not presentable, if not exemplary. I know there are many, both parents and teachers, who pay but little attention to these things, deeming them of but little importance. This negligence is little less than criminal. It is the duty of every teacher and every parent to require as nearly perfect cleanliness in the child as possible. It is necessary that the parent and the teacher set the example. The mother who rises late, and, in her haste to perform her day's duties, puts off the necessary attention to her hair until other work has been disposed of, need not expect to be the happy possessor of model, cleanly children, any more than she need expect herself to be considered a model wife, which God forbid. So, too, the teacher, the corners of whose mouth play the telltale of the filthiness within, or whose boots, upon which the mud of months has been accumulating, have known no polish, can expect nothing better of his pupils. I travelled, a few days ago, in the same car with several members of one of our State Legislatures. Among them was a burly fellow, clad in a plaid shirt of an uncertain color and squirting his tobacco-juice in every direction. As I looked at him, I could not refrain from thinking, if this is one of our representative men, what under the sun must the rest of us look like? And yet this man is the father of a family, and no doubt, like others, shows his best side when away from home.

It is related by a European tourist, in his criticisms on the people of the United States, that on paying a visit to one of our State Legislatures, he found its members "a most untidy set of men." Whether his knowledge of European legislative bodies, or his sense of propriety in matters of dress, led him to make the criticism, or whether the criticism be just or not, I cannot tell; but it is certainly true that too little attention is paid to tidiness in dress. Volumes might be written on this subject, but it concerns us specially only so far as home and school are concerned. Of the dress of society and fashion, its superfluities and its shortcomings, nothing at present need be said.

We are too negligent of dress in the presence of our children. It is the duty of every one to dress neatly, and especially is it the duty of parents and teachers. Did this neatness require unnecessary expense, or tend to beget false pride, it should be heartily condemned. But these are objections which cannot be urged. Neatness and extravagance do not necessarily go together. They are by no means inseparable. Many a mother with her shilling calico shines more brilliantly in her home than another with her expensive silk. It is n't the cost of a dress that makes it either beautiful or comfortable. As I sit at my window, there pass up and down the street before me all classes of persons. I see here the careless and slovenly laborer, with stooping form, body bent forward, hands hanging loosely, gait shambling, and countenance stolid and devoid of all expression. Following immediately and close behind is a no less diligent son of toil; but mark the difference! This man walks upright as God created him, his step is quick and elastic, his clothes show that they, as well as his person, receive proper attention; his countenance beams with good-humor and cheerfulness, which make glad too the heart of the little fellow who trots nimbly at his side. You can read in the very appearance of these two men much of their home-life. You are not surprised to find in the house of the one children and goats disputing possession of the sitting-room, which is often sitting-room, parlor, bed-room, and kitchen in one. There is no such thing as comfort in that home. The children are ragged and unkempt, the mother is a slattern, and the filth and general want of neatness make you glad to get into the open air. You have no desire to visit it again. In the home of the second you find everything bright and cheerful. Neatness and order are apparent in every part. The mother, clad in her working suit, is yet neat; and, as she invites you in, she does n't find it necessary to excuse herself, that she may retire and keep you waiting half an hour, while she prepares to make herself presentable. The children too have caught the spirit of the father and mother, and there is a general neatness about the whole home which makes it an enticing place, and one which the children will leave in the future with sadness and regret.

It is a mistake to suppose that this neatness is to be found in the homes of the wealthy alone, and it is no less a mistake to suppose that either the poor or the rich are the only ones on whom rests the responsibility in this matter. There is a moral question involved in it which affects all classes. We feel that the man who puts up an unsightly building offends us because he offends the public taste, and thus far he has done wrong. So too in the matter of dress. The man or the woman who not only is slovenly in dress, but also by example sends out slovenly children, is guilty of an offence against morality which, though not indictable and punishable by legislative enactment, is nevertheless an offence and indictable by all laws of morality and good taste. The teacher too who permits the pupils of his school to be guilty of this offence, or who, worse still, sets the example by being himself untidy and slovenly in dress, is no less guilty. Let him see to it, when he enters his school-room, that his dress, though it may not be in the prevailing mode, is yet kept neat and clean. His example, like that of the parent, is all-powerful in creating in his pupils habits of neatness.

The personal habits of parents and teachers should be unobjectionable. There is undoubted truth in the maxim: "Example is often more forcible than precept;" and those who expect to instil by precept what their own life contradicts, expect what cannot be accomplished. It is folly for a teacher to think he can establish rules for the guidance of his pupils without showing his own respect for those rules. Thus the teacher who prohibits the use of tobacco and liquor, and yet so far forgets himself as to indulge in using these, proves himself either a very weak man or a hypocrite, and it matters not whether he do this publicly, or, driven by shame, he play both hypocrite and liar in private. If any habit be positively immoral or injurious, the law prohibiting it is binding upon both pupil and teacher. Nothing argues the want of fitness in a man as a moral guide so much as this failure to show by example that the precepts he attempts to instil are righteous. I have no faith in any man whose moral strength is so weak that he cannot support his own rules and regulations, so far as moral grounds are concerned, by his daily example. The father who tells his little boy to abstain from smoking and chewing, and yet smokes and chews unblushingly himself, offers first an inducement to his child to contract the habit by leading him to think that there is something fascinating in it which the father wishes to enjoy by himself; and, secondly, shows the child his own unreasonableness in asking it to abstain from practices which he himself is unwilling to forego. What father is there who would be willing to have his wife and children found, as he often is, at the gaming-table or in a state of intoxication? There are few men who are not anxious to see their children better than themselves.

The teacher's case is analogous. Any practice which he forbids as unbecoming or immoral, he must show to be so by his own life. If he require pupils to assume graceful positions, it does not become him to sit with his feet in the air or on a desk. If he wishes to enforce the criminality of drunkenness and prevent it in his pupils, it is wrong for him to belie his precepts by taking his glass of beer or something stronger in the saloon, though it be for "old acquaintance' sake," and when "no one is there to see." If he require his pupils to abstain from profanity, it ill becomes him, when things go wrong at home, to launch forth a volley of curses at his own wife and children or their awkwardness, even though it be done mentally.

Few dare assert that they are entirely exemplary in their habits. We all plead guilty to being more or less imperfect, but this is not sufficient; we must make amends. In addition to the more serious faults which may be laid to our charge, there are numberless smaller ones in which we might by example do much toward making our children better models than ourselves for future generations to copy after. We require our children to knock before entering a stranger's or a neighbor's door, while we rush thoughtlessly in, sometimes too when we are least expected and least welcome. We advise them to eat slowly and masticate thoroughly, while under the plea of business engagements we bolt our food down with the rapacity of a starved beast, (the reader will pardon the figure if he watches some of our business men dine;) nor does the trouble end here. The difficulty that teachers and parents experience in training their children properly often arises from the fact that they are the unfortunate victims of bad habits contracted in childhood. These habits have become so much the masters of many and have so enslaved them, that it is not without exceedingly great difficulty that they are broken up. Yet, like the troublesome weeds that often infest our most fertile portions of land, they can with the assistance of an energetic spirit be eradicated. "Be ye perfect even as your Father which is in heaven is perfect," is the injunction of the apostle, and we shall have little to fear if we adopt the doctrine.

I cannot close this chapter without referring to the manners and various little courtesies of life which may be best taught at the home fireside or in the school. As I take a stroll down street with my wife, I find an excellent opportunity of ascertaining the culture which many persons have had. As I pass an acquaintance I watch his salute, that I may return it, and at the same time I find out much of his life. Here comes one who, in the bigness of his heart, lifts his hat, and, as he sees me stop, gives me a good hearty greeting; and I read at once the character of the man. Passing a short distance farther, we meet another. This man is in a hurry. He knows nothing but business; so he merely bobs his head mechanically as a fishing-cork bobs under water when jerked vigorously by the fish below, and on he goes. He gives no greeting, says nothing, and you come to the conclusion that he takes no pleasure in society. The next we meet does n't even do us the honor of giving us a salute, but keeps his eyes steadily on my partner, wondering, I suppose, who she can be, and showing at the same time his lack of culture and brains. So in all crowds that we meet when accompanied by ladies, or when ladies are on the streets alone, we find probably one in ten who has gallantry and good breeding enough to lift his hat. The great majority, you will notice, simply give a nod and are gone.

It would be interesting to know just what proportion of these were taught when children, either by example or by precept, to be polite. I recall to mind the time when, as we passed out of the door, each one of the pupils was required to say, "Good evening, sir," to the teacher, and in addition the boys were required to make their bow, while the girls were taught to make a courtesy, as we then called it. Well do I remember, too, how these same girls, when they made their courtesy, added sufficient force, when recovering their perpendicular, to spring from the doorway. Omitting the burlesque part of it, I think it did much good. Some of our most successful teachers, before dismissing school, require their pupils to rise, and, at a second tap of the bell, the teacher and the pupils bow to each other preparatory to passing out. There are many things of this kind which can be taught most effectively both at home and at school by example. The amount of good accomplished, and the confusion and awkwardness avoided by the child in the future, will prove an ample reward for the trouble it may cost.

CHAPTER XII.

HOW SHOULD CHILDREN BE TREATED?

"Well had the boding tremblers learned to trace
The day's disasters in his morning face."

WHENEVER I meet with these lines of Goldsmith's I admit at once their beauty and their truthfulness when applied not only to the schoolmaster at "Auburn, loveliest village of the plain," but to teachers of the present day as well. However much we may attempt to conceal any ill-humor on entering the school for the day, the pupils will find us out, and they will conduct themselves accordingly. Whether they think of it or not, they soon learn, by the general manner of the teacher, to tell when they dare be mischievous without danger, and when it would be unsafe to indulge any such propensity. Much of the teacher's success in school, and much of the parent's at home, in making the life of the child happy, and thus properly prepared to receive instruction and training, depends upon their manner.

Pascal says: "Kind words do not cost much; they never blister the tongue nor lips, and we never heard of any mental trouble arising from this quarter. Though they do not cost much, they help one's good-nature. Soft words soften our own souls. Angry words are fuel to the flame of wrath, and make it burn fiercely. Kind words make other people good-natured. Cold words freeze people, and hot words scorch them, and bitter words make them bitter, and wrathful words make them wrathful. There is such a rush of all other words in our days that it seems desirable to give kind words a chance among them. There are vain words, and idle words, and hasty words, and spiteful words, and empty words, and profane words, and warlike words. Kind words also produce their own image in men's souls, and a beautiful image it is. They quiet and comfort the hearer. They shame him out of his sour, morose, and unkind feelings. We have not yet begun to use kind words in such abundance as they ought to be used." How true this is! How true it is too that these words are the expression of the soul when in its better moods! What reason have we, and what occasion is there for ever speaking to children in any other than a kindly way? Is there not reward for our kindness in the feelings that find expression in words from the little children under our care, when they tell us and tell others that they like to go to school because the teacher is kind and "not cross," as they are wont to express it? Have you never felt glad as one of these little ones handed in her composition on "school," in which, somewhere near the close, she had written, "Our teacher makes us prepare our lessons well, but she is very kind to us." At such a time I have felt that that little sentiment dropped from the lips of an innocent child which knew nothing of flattery, was of more real value than the month's salary.

To take a utilitarian view of the matter, it pays to govern by kindness. The teacher who uses kind words spoken in a kindly manner rarely has occasion to resort to punishment. The teacher who in a surly, snappish manner orders a little boy to close the door will have it closed, and that too in an emphatic manner not to be mistaken; whereas, had his voice and request been kindly, the door would have been closed cheerfully and quietly. Thus with all other requests. We don't expect to find good order in a school-room where the teacher marches around armed with a cherry switch or a ferule, taking more time in issuing such commands as, "Boys, stop that noise!" "John, sit up!" "Don't you hear me there?" "Susan, come up here and stand in the corner!" all of which are poured forth so rapidly that before he has time to see that they are obeyed, both he and his pupils have forgotten them. So too in the family, the parent who governs by kindness receives much more cheerful obedience to his commands than the one who rules by mere force. The mother who is constantly scolding her children finds new difficulties arising every day; whereas, she who rules by kindness, wonders at times why she has such few difficulties to contend with while her neighbors are constantly complaining of unruly children. She makes her home a pleasant place for her children, a hallowed spot around which shall cling sacred memories in the future, when the places that know her now shall know her no more; and the effect is none the less marked because she does this unconsciously and without an effort.

One of the traits which should characterize every parent and teacher is cheerfulness of disposition. It is desirable on their own account as well as on account of their pupils. There are few positions more trying and exhaustive than that of governing children, and anything that will tend to lighten the labor is beneficial. Nothing so much tends to rob teaching of its fatigue as a cheerful spirit. I have gone into school-rooms over which one of these solemn, sour, morose individuals presided, and found things moving along much as we see one smitten with paralysis attempt to walk. Every step seemed to be painful. Every cheerful face had lost its childlike expression, and an ominous soberness of countenance was visible throughout the whole room. There seemed to be no life there. True, this teacher preserved order, but preserved it at the expense of the child's happiness. There was n't a child in the room on which the effects of this system were not noticeable. Mark the contrast presented when you enter a room presided over by a teacher brimful of life and cheerfulness. You hear a hum and continuous buzz throughout the room, but it is the buzz that one hears as he enters a manufactory. It means work. Now and then the teacher enjoys a hearty laugh with his pupils. He sees less harm in having a laugh now and then than in penning up the flow of life in the child and having it steal its opportunities. How many of us are there who must plead guilty if a hearty laugh in school were criminal? The teacher who desires to make his school a pleasant and inviting place, must be cheerful, ready not only to laugh himself, but ready also to enjoy a laugh with his boys and girls. I can imagine no more disagreeable place to a child than a school-room presided over by one of these non-laughing people! The parents also in the family circle must be cheerful. It should be their aim to make home as pleasant a place as possible, that it may be attractive to their children. I like the home and the school in which music is heard. When music bursts out spontaneously, the heart is full and overflowing. It then becomes a fit exponent of the cheerfulness that is reigning within. Let the song be heard in the home often.

Parents and teachers should possess the Christian virtue of patience. We all in our daily occupations find occasion for the exercise of this virtue, but no one probably feels the necessity of being supported by it more than the mother in her family or the teacher in the school. Children are more or less thoughtless, and though not guilty of doing wrong intentionally, they often cause trouble which taxes the patience of those in charge of them. Let me instance a case or two. A little child, with the kindest intentions in the world, drops a plate and breaks it. The impatient mother at once loses her temper, and must indulge herself in a good hearty scold. She is out of humor for a whole day. The mother who is patient, well knowing that the child is already in a measure punished by his own feelings of sorrow, instead of indulging in a violent outbreak of temper, soothes the child, and in a few moments makes it forget its sadness. Which of the two causes the child to be more careful in the future? Certainly not the former. In the school-room, some luckless little urchin in a moment of forgetfulness infringes one of the rules of the school. Our patient man pays but little attention to the matter; for he sees that however much it may interfere with the good order, it was not an offence, because not intentional, and he dismisses the child with a single word of caution. The impatient teacher would have called up the little fellow immediately and given him a severe whipping or its equivalent, without stopping to inquire as to his guilt. Thus, day after day, both the parent and the teacher meet with numberless little things calculated to tax their patience almost to the last degree of endurance. We may feel that we are accomplishing little good; but when we least expect it, we shall find the bread we have cast upon the waters return to us. Be patient with the children you have in your charge. They are frail creatures, and like ourselves fallible. Were you, fond mother, deprived of a single one of them to-morrow, you would reproach yourself for your harsh and unkind treatment of that one when under the influence of excitement. Think not so much of your own comfort as of the importance and welfare of that human soul which God has placed in your care for guidance.

There is on the part of parents and teachers very frequently what might be termed a lack of gentleness, and, singular as it may seem, it is not confined to those in the lower walks of life. I have seen petulant outbreaks of temper in those claiming to be the most refined, which were anything but creditable. Of course the basis of this is mainly a lack of patience and self-control. Few parents stop to think how unpleasant they are making their homes by this sort of treatment of their children. The little ones skulk away into the corners or slyly slip out of the house to escape from the danger. Such harsh and inhuman treatment of the child does much toward hardening it and making it rebellious. It lives under a continual fear that some little mishap or indiscretion may bring down the storm upon its head. A little boy once remarked to me: "Our teacher last winter was scolding continually; he never knew when to quit talking." On inquiring whether he secured good order in this way, the boy replied: "Oh, no! we all did as we pleased. When we wanted to lie down on the benches or put our feet on the desks, we did so. We had everything our own way." Is this not in general the result of scolding, both in the school-room and in the home? Is it not a fact beyond denial that those who make the greatest bluster and noise generally accomplish the least? Independent of this result, gentleness in the teacher or the parent begets a corresponding gentleness in the child. Have you never noticed the little girl as she plays with her doll, or the little boy as he drives his imaginary horse, that each imitates your manner? If your manner is rude, theirs is rude; if gentle, they are also gentle. It is but the influence of the home example.

Were I to sum up the treatment of the child, I could give no better comprehensive rule than the one so often quoted: "Do unto others as you would have others do unto you." Suppose yourself, for the moment, assuming the place of the child, what treatment would you desire?

Having settled this in your mind, you are prepared to decide what treatment is due the child, and therefore best calculated to make its life pleasant and profitable. Were you to select an instructor or a companion by whom you would wish to be influenced, it would not be one who is dogged, sullen, sour, morose, and impatient, but one who, on the contrary, is lively, cheerful, kind, patient, gentle, pleasant, and obliging. Your child needs this same kind of instructor.

CHAPTER XIII.

GOVERNMENT.

I DO not propose to discuss here the subject of government at length, nor do I propose to present a system of ethics. My space for that would prove too limited, and it would not comport with the object I have in view, that of presenting to the reader a few practical hints in a familiar way. I shall deal with government only so far as it relates to the family and the school, as that is all that specially concerns us at present.

Every well-digested and well-balanced system of government has affixed a system of rewards and punishments — rewards for well-doing, and punishments for offences. It is so with all laws, whether physical, civil, or moral. Every infringement of a physical law is punished with pain or ill health, and either through neglect or through ignorance of these laws thousands almost daily are hurried off to eternity. Each civil law has its penalty attached, and when obedience is denied, the offender suffers the penalty. So too in the infringement of a moral law, we know that if we refuse obedience we must suffer the punishment ordained of God. Thus when the revealed law of God tells us that the drunkard shall not inherit the kingdom of heaven, there is at once a command prohibiting drunkenness, and at the same time the penalty of disobedience is made known. God speaks to us through the Scriptures in no uncertain terms. The law and the penalty are there both set forth.

Family government and school government, which are much the same — the teacher during a part of the day simply taking the place of the parent — embrace to a great extent both the civil and the moral law; hence, from the nature of these two kinds of government, what will apply to the one must, so far as fundamental principles are concerned, apply to the other; and as the parental relation takes precedence, let us first consider family government, and we shall have at once that which embraces both. It is not a mere agency, but in truth a government in which there are rules and laws to be obeyed and authority to be maintained. Some of the principles which must regulate this government have been spoken of in the preceding chapters. We have proved that this government does not consist in the brutish harshness which is apt to prevail at times, nor yet in that looseness which permits the child such absolute freedom that it soon establishes itself as monarch of the household. The latter too plainly argues the absence of government, just as the former ignores its fundamental principles.

One of the first principles of family, as of all other kinds of government, is that there must be a well-adapted system of rewards and punishments. Each offence should have its proper penalty attached, and, when properly administered, such punishment should be inflicted as is naturally suited to the offence. We would have little faith in the doctor who for consumption, dyspepsia, toothache, neuralgia, fever, and all other ills, should prescribe cod-liver oil. Though it might be beneficial in some cases, we would not be willing to acknowledge it as a panacea for all ills, otherwise we should need no physician. But this physician's course were no more unwise than our own when we apply the same corrective in every case of moral disease, the only change we make being in the size of the doses. You, Mr. A., believe in corporal punishment, and you quote Solomon in support of your theory and belief. When your child tells a lie, you whip it; when it breaks a pitcher, you whip it; when it loses a piece of money or its knife, you whip it; when it disobeys, you whip it; and for every other offence your punishment is whipping. Madam B., you do not believe in whipping. When your child is careless, you shut it in the closet; when it plays truant, you shut it in the closet; when in its play it leaves the floor strewn with bits of paper or sticks, you pick them up, and shut it in the closet. Shutting in the closet is your panacea for all moral ills. Your panacea, Mrs. C., is reproof. When your child is too slow in its work, you scold it; when it calls its playfellow a thief or fights with him, you scold it; when it is idle, or when by carelessness it injures the furniture, you scold it. And so for every other offence you scold your child. You call it reproof; but you know that scolding is generally a fitter name for your way of administering this reproof. Each one of you has a special mode of punishing, and each one fails; but your neighbor, who boasts that he never punishes, fails with you. It is true he never punishes; but it is true too that there is no government in his family; for his children are not angels, as you probably have occasion to know. The great mistake in each of the three cases is, that the same punishment, though in different degrees, is meted out to offences differing not only in magnitude but differing still more widely in their nature. There is no visible relation between the offence and the penalty; and thus the first fundamental principle of government is ignored.

There is a natural relationship existing between the offence and the proper penalty; but the parent often makes no effort to trace out this relation. Let me instance a few cases to show what I mean. Suppose your child has been amusing itself on the floor, and while engaged in play has scattered bits of paper or pieces of rag over the carpet. In its haste to get at something else when it has become tired of this play, it runs away, leaving the floor in a sad condition. What is the proper punishment for its carelessness? Shall it be whipped, scolded, shut in the closet, or sent to bed without its supper? Which of these bears any relation to the offence? Not one of them. The proper thing to do in the case is to require the child, before proceeding to any other play, to clear up the matter it has left on the floor, and set things in order as they were before it commenced its play. Thus while it sees at once the connection between the offence and the punishment, it at the same time forms habits of neatness and order. The mother who would do this work for the child, though she might mean it as a great kindness, would be doing it a great wrong. Suppose another case. A child habitually abuses privileges granted to it. When permitted to walk on the pavement, with the injunction to go no further, it runs into the street, or when granted other privileges, it goes further than these extend. Shall we punish it by any bodily infliction, or resort to scolding? However much reproof may benefit it, evidently the first punishment is to deprive it of all such privileges until it shows signs of penitence; and the natural penalty attached should be understood. In this manner parents will be able to strengthen their authority, while at the same time the child knows the penalty before violating a law.

As a general rule, when any damage is done, the offender should be required to make reparation. Thus when any one breaks a window-pane at the school-house, he should be required to replace it or pay for the glass and the setting of it. If he throw paper or other material on the floor, it is proper that he should be made to pick it up again. If he make a spittoon of the floor, it is right that he should be made to clean it up. If he carry in mud on his boots, he should sweep it out again. If he abuse his playmates, he should be debarred from their company. In each case he sees the relation between the punishment and the offence.

It will be admitted on all sides that our family government is often defective, and that well-regulated families are the exceptions, not the rule. In too many households of the land the order has been reversed, and the children are in too many cases the rulers. I am aware that this seems a strong assertion, yet is it not the case that children are allowed to do as they please? A mistaken kindness on the part of the parent leads him into this error, and before he is aware of it his authority is lost and set at defiance. This argues the lack of qualifications necessary to govern. Carrying this matter to the school-room, how rarely do we hear it said of a teacher that he is an excellent disciplinarian!

I am here brought to a point of which I have before spoken, that of educating our young men and women for the position they will be required to hold as parents. When we look at this matter as we should, we begin to understand just why it is that our family government is so defective. How absurd it seems when we think of the time when a man to be a tailor was required to apprentice himself for a term of seven years; and yet when he came to be married or take charge of a school he was supposed to be fit to govern and instruct children without any previous training! That is, it took seven years to learn to make a coat or a pair of pantaloons, but to train a human being for this life and immortality any one was supposed to be competent on arriving at the age of manhood. How much better than this is the matter now? True, we have Normal Schools for the professional training of teachers; but how many avail themselves of the opportunities offered there? and where are our schools for the training of parents? or where are our schools of any kind in which young men and young women are ever spoken to specially on this subject? The mad theorist may call all this base utilitarianism, but the fact still stares him in the face that unless we mend the matter our family government will grow no better, and it may grow much worse.

Were I attempting here to write a scientific work, I might go on to enumerate a great number of disqualifications which unfit one for securing good family government, but such is not my design at all; and for those I shall have to refer the reader to works on ethics, where the matter is treated more at length. I may say here, however, that a natural affection for children, unless warily regulated, is by no means the only nor the most important qualification. I acknowledge its great power; but when not guided and guarded by prudence, it is apt at times to run into error. To prove this, it is only necessary to notice the real cruelties perpetrated in the way of mistaken kindness in helpless infancy.

One of the prominent characteristics of true family government is, that we should not govern or refuse to govern because it may just at that time be in accordance with our humor or suit our convenience. The law of right must direct us in all cases. We are not permitted to drop into a listless, irresponsible way, and decide a point just as it may happen to suit our convenience or pleasure. A desire to have our children noticed, to have them appear manly and womanly, often leads us into indiscretions that may serve to ruin them. Often, too, we defer such government as is necessary, because our humor may for the time not be suited by such a course

12*

as duty requires. It may too at times, especially in the presence of others, not be pleasant to do our whole duty, particularly in administering punishment. How soon the little folks learn this! Seeing that the mother or the teacher finds it so unpleasant a duty to reprove or punish them in the presence of strangers that it is rarely attempted, they generally manage to have things their own way at such times. The principle is wrong. If punishment at such times becomes necessary it should be administered. No improper influences or bad motives should be permitted to interfere.

There should be perfect unity of sentiment in those having authority. On this point hear what Dr. Tiersch in his treatise on the Christian Family Life says: "A wife cannot weaken the authority of the father without undermining her own; for her authority rests upon his, and if that of the mother is subordinated to that of the father, yet it is but one authority, which cannot be weakened in either of the two who bear it without injury to both. The mother, therefore, must consider it a matter of family decorum which is not to be broken, never, even in little matters, to contradict the father in the presence of the children, except with the reservation of a modest admission of his right of decision, and that in cases which admit of no delay. But just as much is it the duty of the husband to leave the authority of his wife unassailed in the presence of other members of the household; and when he is obliged to overrule her objections, to do it in a tender and kindly form. If he turns to her with roughness and harshness from jealousy of his place of rule, it is not only the heart of his wife which is estranged from him; with the children too intervenes a weakening of the moral power, under which they should feel themselves placed. If in their presence their mother is blamed as foolish or obstinate, and so lowered to the place of a child or a maid-servant, that sanctity immediately vanishes which, in the eyes of the children, surrounds the heads of both father and mother in common." Thus by constant disagreements between father and mother, all authority will in the end be lost, and the children will either lose much respect for both, or they will be divided into factions, one adhering to the father and the other to the mother, as the affection for the one or the other may predominate. But if this harmony of purpose is necessary between the parents, it argues at once that it is also important and necessary between parents and teachers; and here rests the most important argument in favor of parental coöperation with the teacher, that the child may be properly governed and educated. The father and the mother should just as soon listen to the silly twaddle it may indulge in against each other, as the tales it may carry home and tell against its teacher. Nothing so much cripples the authority and power of the teacher as a lack of this coöperation and sympathy of parents.

In general it is best to make no threat which you do not mean to carry out. The parent or teacher who tries to govern by threatening to break the necks of his children or cut off their ears, does n't gain any better control of them. Children soon learn to measure such threats and estimate them at their proper value, as being simply so many empty words. In fact the policy of making any threats at all is one of doubtful expediency, as it generally argues a cowardly heart. The habit of making these threats is so easily contracted that in a short time one becomes so much addicted to it that they bear with them no force whatever and simply make falsifiers of us. If, however, a threat is indiscreetly made to punish a child in a certain manner for disobedience, the man who has any regard for his word is bound to carry it out. Let him try this, and see how soon he will be in a dilemma.

Let me here urge a word against the policy of frightening children. How vividly I recall to mind some of the remarkable stories I used to hear when sitting in the village store, of spooks, and ghosts, and blue-lights, of headless men and men with terrible eyes! And when I went to my home after hearing these, although it was but a few rods distant, I used to run with a speed that I was unable to summon at any other time, expecting every moment to be gobbled up by one of these supernatural monsters. Alas! how many of us have suffered by the indiscretion of those who told us these hobgoblin stories! How many of us now go through lonely places at night as calmly as we would in daylight, and as calmly as we would had we never been frightened? How many are there of my readers who even now venture into the cellar at night as fearlessly as they do to their couches? It is not caution that makes us hesitate so much as it is fear. On this special ground, I think the punishment of confining children in dark rooms a dangerous one. They should never be frightened. These ridiculous ghost-stories, if necessary to be told at all, which is doubtful, they should never hear until they are old enough to know them to be pure fabrications and silly. Our plan should be wiser than that which made us for a time superstitious.

Children should be made to feel that in all government the one who exercises authority over them is their friend. It is a mistake to suppose that through the fear we inspire we gain greater authority. A single cheerful act of obedience is worth more than a dozen of the same acts through fear. There is a time too when this fear ceases to have any force, to say nothing of the tendency such discipline has to make children deceitful; whereas such government as is secured through friendship is firm not only during school-days but in all after-life.

The child should understand that the parent means just what he says, and that there is no vacillating. In other words, the parent and the teacher should be firm. There should be no yielding when in the right. With this firmness of course can be united mildness and kindness; but the child should learn from the beginning that when the parent says no, he means no, and when he says yes, he means yes. Parents and teachers, do you never, when you have denied your child a certain privilege, in a half-hour afterward, when feeling in a better humor and less annoyed, grant him the same privilege? How many of you can conscientiously answer no? How many of you, after having ordered a child not to do a certain thing, still allow him to do it without correction? It is a delicate question, I know, and I will not press it; but let me ask you to think of the influence this vacillating conduct will have on your child.

There is no more dangerous policy pursued than that of constantly issuing commands and prohibitions, and yet failing to pay any further attention to them. Children can be governed much more readily by speaking less and making fewer rules. Sometimes from morning to night they are cautioned and commanded not to do this and prohibited from doing that, until they believe themselves thoroughly sinful and inclined to do everything on which the seal of prohibition is stamped. All this talk is unnecessary, and it accomplishes nothing.

The parent who hopes to make his family government at once pleasant, simple, and effective, must trust his children. They are not by any means so vicious in their nature as some would have you believe, unless that viciousness is engendered by your own mistaken way of governing. If your example has been a proper one, which is all-important in government, and you are willing to trust your children, you will rarely find them other than trustworthy.

CHAPTER XIV.

PUNISHMENTS.

IN nothing does the government in different families differ so much as in the method of punishment. In some families we find ardent supporters of the punishment system, while in others punishment is tabooed, and children are governed by the law of love. I do not propose to argue here which hold the proper ground. I have no doubt objections could be found to the arguments of both, nor have I any doubt that a commingling of the two systems would probably prove much the most effective means of securing good discipline.

I believe in the efficacy of kindness in governing; but when, under the plea of love, I find a whole family of children running to ruin, and shoving their impertinence into every one's face, I begin to think that possibly there is not so much love there as the fond parents would have us think. I begin to suspect that that family of children have had their own way so much that neither father nor mother has as much control over them as is necessary for their welfare, or they have not trained them to respect any other authority than their own. I have met children of this kind who were governed so much by the law of love, and were so seldom corrected, that I have found them setting all authority at defiance. On the other hand, I have met those too who have been governed entirely by force, and I would do the former injustice were I to say that these impressed me any more favorably. There are those who never from one week's end to another expect to hear a kind word in the homestead or in the school-room, and they are not disappointed. They do not look for anything but cuffs, and kicks, and harsh words, and hence are always prepared to receive them, and forget them as soon as received. I have known such to grow up to manhood, hardened men and ready for almost any wickedness, and I do not wonder at this at all; for it is the legitimate fruit of such a method of government. It isn't because there was anything evil in the heart of the boy that he received these oft-repeated punishments, but a purely petulant spirit on the part of the parent or teacher. You will understand then that my theory, whether correct or not, is, that punishment and the law of love must both be resorted to in order to govern children properly. So long as love is supported by the authority to punish, but little difficulty will be experienced; but if the child once learn that the parent does not sanction punishment under any circumstances, then will it soon assume under peculiar temptations to govern itself. I believe too that in a well-governed family, as in a well-governed school, it is rarely necessary to resort to punishment, and especially corporal punishment; for it is seldom you find children so vicious that they commit acts of wilful disobedience if their training from earliest infancy has been properly attended to; and yet back of this government must stand the power of enforcing obedience. There are those, I know, who hold that this authority need not exist, but that by mere kindness the child can and should always be governed; and yet I have no knowledge of one of these who does so govern, that does not at least indulge now and then in a hearty scold. How much more they claim for this than for punishment of some kind wherein they do not disgrace themselves and set the child an evil example, I am unable to say.

In the infliction of punishments we must be both just and merciful. Jean Paul says: "Not great but unavoidable punishments are mighty, truly almighty." When it is necessary to inflict punishment, it should be inflicted only to such an extent as fulfils the ends of justice, no more. The parent who for the mere pleasure of the thing, or the gratification it may afford him, chastises or punishes a child to an unnecessary extent, is cruel, and very properly makes himself liable to indictment by process of civil law. How many there are who thus inhumanly thrash and cudgel their children until at last these latter are glad when the day comes for their departure from the homestead! Is it any wonder? They are not so treated by strangers; and it is no wonder that they are glad to leave home, nor that they long for the day when all this petty tyranny shall cease to be exercised over them. Far better it is for the child to feel that you have punished it less than it deserves, than to feel that it has been unjustly and cruelly punished.

A second principle which should govern us in punishing is, that we must inquire narrowly into the nature of the offence committed and the causes that may have led to it. Until we understand all these things, we are not prepared to administer punishment either justly or mercifully. How often do we see one of these blustering, nervous, fidgety sort of people enter a school-room, and from morn to night move around among the little children armed with a strap or a switch, always prepared to deal out blows without stint and without question! If it ever was your ill-fortune to be under the charge of such a teacher, you, doubtless, bear him no special love to-day. Few pupils respect the authority of such a teacher. True, most of them obey; but not from respect, and when school-life is over, they look back on their school-days with anything but pleasure. Aside, however, from the disrespect which is engendered after a time, children who are thus constantly punished become accustomed to it, and from that moment it is of none effect. Some of the worst boys, though not naturally so, that I have ever known, are those who were accustomed to receive punishment almost as regularly as their meals; and in every such case I have found the best mode of treatment to be directly the opposite of that to which they had been subjected at home. If parents understood this matter better and were less inclined to consult the fickle whims of their own temper, we might hope for much more good. Here is where the trouble lies. Of course teachers are to blame in a measure too, and I would not consciously lift the responsibility from the shoulders of any one on whom God may have placed it.

No one is prepared to inflict punishment justly when

angry. I know what a difficult matter it is, when thrown off our guard by something either positively wrong or detrimental to the general good order, to keep proper control over our temper, and resist the consequent temptation to inflict punishment immediately. But this is one of the trials to which parents and teachers are subjected. There is danger of doing great injustice when punishment is administered in anger. We have no time to inquire into the circumstances that may have led to the commission of the offence, and these may in some cases be such as wholly to obviate the necessity of any punishment. In punishing when we are angry, we feel too much disposed to gratify the demands of our own unreasonableness, and thus administer a greater punishment than the nature of the offence demands. Almost every case of punishment that results in bodily injury to the child is a case in which the punishment has been administered in anger. There is, on the other hand, if we defer the punishment until our anger has subsided, no danger of dealing unjustly with the child. It is, as I have before stated, much better to punish too little than too much; for generally it is not the pain that is so much dreaded by the child as it is the disgrace of being punished. When the punishment is inflicted in anger, the proper effect is lost. Instead of a feeling of sorrow for its fault and a real desire to do better, the child fosters the anger which it finds responding to that of the teacher or parent, and promises itself full reparation and vengeance for the degradation it has been made to suffer. Thus, viewed on all sides and from every imaginable stand-point, it is objectionable. As a safe guide, let me say, the teacher or parent should always defer punishment until he is perfectly cool and prepared to punish only so far as is positively necessary.

When punishment is inflicted, the child should understand that it is an unpleasant task to perform, and that those who administer it do so with regret. It should feel that we punish it from a desire to make it better and at the same time to fulfil our duty to it and to its Maker. No after anger should be permitted to enter into our hearts. Shutting the child away from us only goes to prove that our anger is not yet sated, and exposes at once the falsity of our discipline. How beautifully does Richter express it when he says: "Fear and hatred of the punishment, which at first hardened and struggled against what was said, are now past, and gentle instruction falls in and heals, as honey relieves a sting and oil cures wounds. During this hour one may speak much if the gentlest possible tone of voice be used, and soften the grief of others by showing our own. But every long winter of after-wrath is poisonous; at most an after-grief, not an after-punishment, is allowable."

The object of punishment is never degradation, and any punishment which has for its object either degradation or torture is both wrong and sinful. It only serves to harden the heart of the child, and accomplishes no good. Therefore all such punishments as those barbarous ones of making a child hold a book at arm's length, kneel on peas, "hold a nail in the floor," stand on one foot, together with the wearing of dunce-caps and old bonnets, standing on a stool (which degrades while it elevates), with numberless others of a similar nature, are all wrong and out of place. Many of the old kinds of punishment in vogue thirty years ago or more were of this character; and it seems to me sometimes now yet, when I read over the regulations of a Board of Directors requiring teachers to whip on the hand of the child only, that the barbarity of the past methods has not yet been wholly lost. How horrible the punishment inflicted by those old teachers who used to make us place our finger-ends together, and with the first stroke of the ferule almost burst the nails from their places! It makes one's flesh creep yet to think of their cruelty; but the culture of the times, they thought, demanded it. Possibly it did, but there is no such excuse for us of the present. What knowledge we have added to theirs should enable us to do better, and though no less just, be more merciful and humane.

CHAPTER XV.

HOW TO GET WORK OUT OF CHILDREN.

THERE is that in the heading of this chapter which may at first thought startle the reader. I have been at a loss to put any other heading, however, under which the principles I desire to explain might be embraced. Don't therefore be startled at the subject. I am by no means an advocate of that utilitarianism which makes of either man or child a "beast of burden." You look about, possibly at the hour of six or after in the evening, and all around you see men bowed together with toil rapidly hurrying to their homes. A few of these seem happy and cheerful; for the day's work is done, and they know the pleasures that await them at the home fireside; and as they near the doorway, glad little beings run out to meet them and tell them all the news of the day. But a great portion of these workmen are gloomy; their eyes are bent to the ground, and they know but little pleasure in this life save that falsely named which they glean in the beer saloon or at the wine-cup. I believe in work, and in the dignity of labor and the laborer, but I can see no dignity in drudgery nor in the drudge. I believe that we all have our special work to perform, but this work is noble; it is not drudgery. There are few callings in the world that are not honorable, but to make them dignified we must adapt ourselves to them. The aristocrat may pass you by because you are simply a clerk, a teacher, a milliner, or a mechanic; but he only shows the littleness and meanness of his own soul. The dainty miss whose father is a lawyer or a millionaire merchant may refuse to associate with your young folks and sneer at their common dress; but the soul of one pure, simple-hearted Christian boy or girl would make the balance "kick the beam," though weighed down by a thousand of the other.

The fond parent who trains up his children to abhor labor or regard it as degrading has already done much to ruin them. It is a mistaken notion that because we possess a goodly share of money or property, we can therefore sit down and idly fold the hands to enjoy the fruits of our patrimony. I have no respect for an idler. Work is our destiny, and only by it are we disciplined for the enjoyment of what is in store for us in the future. Our world is a working world. Men and women all around us everywhere are at work. Each has his special sphere. One gleans the fruits of the tropics while another gathers those of the farm; while one stands on the engine and rushes with scream and clatter through the forests and over the plains, with the lives of a hundred human beings in his hands, another stands between the shafts of his wheelbarrow loaded with stones or dirt, and trundles it up and down a plank; while one sits in the executive chair, and moulds and directs the destiny of a state or a nation, another rules and directs the movements of a family or a school. But with all this work there must of course be some play. This then is the kind of work in which we must engage: a work which, while it enables us to accomplish much good, yet permits us to share the enjoyments of life.

There is a difference in the manner in which children perform work. While one goes to his task with a light, merry, and cheerful heart, another never does anything that is required of him without grumbling and muttering out his protests. While one sings, the other grumbles. One esteems his work as nothing; the other looks upon his condition as slavish and intolerable. The former finishes his work in a magical sort of way, without any visible exertion and in the best of humor, while the latter wearies and worries over it, and accomplishes the task only with the greatest difficulty and fatigue. Where does the cause of this difference lie? Partly in the heart, in the natural disposition of the child, you say. True, it lies partly in this, but much more in the training and treatment these children have received. One has always been accustomed to perform his work cheerfully and the other reluctantly. The peculiar disposition of the child in either case has been strengthened until there seems no longer any possibility of correcting the fault.

There is a feeling among many parents that they have a right to require work from their children to any extent and in whatever manner they please. Probably they have, but they must not feel surprised and chagrined when they fail to command the respect of the public and fail also in their government. When we come to examine narrowly into the manner of asking children or, it may be, compelling them to perform any task, we no longer wonder why obedience is yielded sometimes so reluctantly. The slave who has dangling over his naked back the cruel lash of his yet more cruel overseer's whip, bears his taskmaster but little love, nor would we under similar circumstances do any better. Few of us believe in the doctrine of coercion when milder means are at hand, if we are the subjects for treatment. Nothing so quickly aggravates us as to have the clenched fist shaken in our face! Why should we expect the child to be more reasonable than ourselves? It is certain then that we accomplish nothing in the way of securing work, and I mean mental work as well as physical, by being hard taskmasters.

There is a rule which may be applied as an effectual guide in every case. Let praise, not censure, be your governing power. Notice how this continual fault-finding hardens the child. Day after day he hears nothing drop from the lips of either parents or teacher but expressions like these: "You are a very bad boy!" "You are the most careless child I ever saw!" "You are a real good-for-nothing little fellow!" and dozens more of the same sort. What must be the effect of all such censure? Certainly we can expect no child to love and respect us for such treatment. We have no right thus to be continually looking on the dark side of things. The child is compelled to live in a sort of poisonous atmosphere which sours his disposition. All blossoming sentiments of confidence and esteem are blighted. It becomes morose and sullen, and never goes to work cheerfully, but more

> "like the quarry slave at night,
> Scourged to his dungeon."

What is the effect of praise, on the other hand? Notice with what alacrity a little fellow who is accustomed to being praised goes about his work! You put a task before him which you think is almost beyond his strength, but he goes at it and begins as if he meant to overcome it; and as he works, thrilling little melodies burst from his lips that bespeak the gladness and glee that are reigning within. Do you say that this whistling betokens a vacant mind, an empty head? Give me that mind rather than that of the aged and venerable scholar who has none of this sunshine in his heart. That boy has a reward in the praise he receives which is far greater and more valuable to him than the pittance of money you pay; and he goes at his work as God meant he should. I envy his feelings almost; and who shall say that his work in life, spreading joy around him wherever he goes, is not as acceptable to God as is that of the sedate, dignified, and solemn sage who says: "The boy hath a devil in his heart; that whistling betokens an empty mind." Who of us would not rather in this case be the innocent, happy child than the bilious professor, however many honors may rest on his head? Let us then praise the child whenever we can, never resorting to censure unless it becomes an absolute necessity. I believe that it is sometimes necessary to censure, but such occasions are rare if we adopt the policy of praising the child when we find praise due. Our own experience in this matter might be an excellent guide. We know how little we respect that authority which attempts to force us into compliance with any measure, and how much that which gives us our due measure of credit, not to say praise, for every act we perform. We know too how rebellious we are apt to become when forced, and how gladly we perform an act for which we receive praise. It is more valuable to us than money. Our children do not differ from us materially. They are, like ourselves, human, with all the feelings and sentiments of human beings.

A story is somewhere related which illustrates in a measure the treatment here referred to.* "Two stages," it is said, "belonging to opposite lines, left the same place at the same hour every day for London. Both drivers had orders to make the distance in the shortest time possible. One driver mounted the box, with whip in hand, was excited, spoke angrily to his horses, and alternately relaxed and jerked the reins, at the same time using his whip freely. In a few miles his horses gave signs of distress, and before he had reached London some of his team were usually broken down. The other driver coolly took his seat, spoke gently to his horses, held a steady rein all the time, and seldom even cracked his whip. He was often hindmost for a few miles, but while the horses of the other team were in a foam, hardly a hair of his horses was moist. The last few miles, his team not being jaded, he took the lead, and seldom even distressed a horse." Who has not seen the same difference nearer

* Dr. Plumer.

home, not only in the management of horses, but in the government of children as well? To apply the theory in another case, the same may be said of the treatment of servants. We hear continual complaints that we no longer can get any good servants, and in many households the first of each succeeding month does not come more regularly than the usual dismission of the servant. Why all this? Is it always the servant that is in fault? True, many of them may be careless; but is our treatment of them always what it should be? Are we under no obligations to them? We may not esteem their position as high as our own, but then that does not by any means lift from our shoulders the responsibilities we have assumed in becoming their masters and employers. They are obliged to be faithful, careful, and obedient, and for this we pay them; but, on the other hand, we are under obligations to be kind, to make their positions comfortable, and above all to avoid censuring where it is not positively demanded. Three-fourths of all the trouble in those cases in which servants become independent and presumptuous might thus be avoided. A servant treated properly, receiving praise where it is her due, kindly and patiently shown how to correct what she may have done amiss, and indulged in that pleasure which is necessary to her mental and moral well-being, will grow to love her mistress, and all cause for quarrel will be avoided. No, the trouble is not all with the servants until they have been hardened by unjust and unkind treatment. If we make an application of this same principle in the school-room, it will be the most certain means of securing not only good order but also cheerful obedience to all the requirements of the school. The teacher, as also the parents, should not, however, let this praise merge into untruthfulness or flattery. There is no necessity for bringing in falsehood to our assistance. There are so many little acts occurring daily which merit our praise, that it is difficult to see how any one can well withhold it when it is so easily given. Well do I remember how one of my latest teachers won the hearts of his pupils by thanking them for every little act of kindness they performed. When we handed him a book or a pencil during recitation, he never failed to thank us; and I know that more apples were piled on that teacher's desk through his thanks than by his instruction. It was a pleasure to do him a favor.

Before closing this chapter, I must add a word on the policy of giving children at times something to do for themselves. Nothing seems to be the source of more pleasure to them than those things which they can call their own. I believe therefore that as soon as boys are prepared to use and take proper care of them, they should be furnished with a work-bench and a set of tools. How many there are to-day who have n't the requisite mechanical skill even to drive a nail, from the lack of opportunity to practise in youth! So also girls should be furnished with a complete sewing outfit — basket, needles, scissors, and all included. Don't jump at the conclusion that I want them to work continually with these. I mean them as a reward for services rendered cheerfully. Should you be so fortunate as to live where you have plenty of tillable ground, I know of nothing that will at once be so pleasing and so beneficial to them as a share in the estate. That is, give to each one a little flower-bed, or garden patch to take care of, and allow them all to make whatever use of the products they may see fit. If they choose to give them to the poor or to sell them, let them do so. They will take a much greater pride in this patch of ground and in attending to it carefully than one would suppose, and at the same time they gain much valuable knowledge, and contract habits that will adhere to them through life. There is nothing a boy covets so much as this starting out in business for himself while under the guiding eye of his parents. I sometimes think that much improvement would soon be manifested by the adoption of a plan of this kind, especially in the taste displayed in laying out grounds and ornamenting and beautifying homes. If it accomplished nothing more than this it would be invaluable: but it would also serve to throw a charm around home-life of which too many homes are now devoid, and obedience to all commands and requests would be both more cheerful and more prompt.

CHAPTER XVI.

MORAL CULTURE.

STRANGE as it may seem, that education which is to fit man for the most important duties of this life as well as for the enjoyments of the rewards and pleasures of the eternal life to follow, receives the least attention. While daily lessons are recited in the various branches of intellectual study, while pupils day after day are instructed how to exercise their physical powers most beneficially, while every effort is made to impart such practical instruction as will enable them to count up the interest on their bank-notes and calculate their loss and gain in business, or teach them the shortest route to Greenland or New Zealand, nothing in the way of formal training of the moral powers is attempted. Indeed, among parents, those upon whom rests the greatest responsibility in this matter, often little attention is paid to the subject.

I do not believe that man can be trained truly intellectually without being trained morally, nor can there be such a physical culture as God designs us to have, without heart-training as well. True, much of our system of education seems to ignore this culture, and we speak of carrying a young man through college or through the university without paying any attention to his moral training. But so may we also take a bundle of nerves, and fibres, and bones, and sinews, and toughen them to the tenacity of steel, but we have not produced a symmetrical specimen of manhood. It is hard to tell what name we ought to apply in the case of purely intellectual education. I know of no word in our language that would serve as a name for it. In the case of pure physical culture, we have produced little more than a brute, a shoulder-hitter, a prize-fighter. The purely intellectual produces men without consciences; men who live that they may grow rich, who accumulate their wealth through the privations, trials, and sufferings of their employees; who coin the very sweat of their workmen into gold. It gives us too our political sharks and tricksters. We have been too long afflicted with the fruits of this culture. Men without honesty, integrity, and the other cardinal virtues, are working all around us. Everywhere their lank, bony fingers are drawing in the gold or clutching the clasps of the public purse.

Does any one question the necessity of more method in our moral culture? Let him consult the statistics of our almshouse and prison reports. Let him visit the dens in our larger towns and cities. Let him enter some of our legislative halls, and see the corruption that everywhere stalks abroad. Day after day we are compelled to look upon pictures of degradation in politics, which are sufficient to bring the indignant blush to the cheek of every honest man. The morality of office-hunting has indeed sunk so low that our best men are loth to be found in the company of wire-working politicians. There are, of course, honorable exceptions, and these are worthy of our highest regard and most implicit confidence; but unfortunately for the public, the weak ones who fall an easy prey to the tempter are neither few nor inactive. The political axes to be ground are effective weapons in destroying public morals. Not competency, but the ability to return a political favor, too often decides the selection of candidates. What is the cause of all this? Evidently it is the strongest argument that can be urged in favor of more methodical moral culture.

There is no doubt that much of the crime that we find chronicled in the public press arises from a defective system of moral culture. Children too often are permitted to train themselves. The mind of the child is pliant and impressible, and too great care cannot be exercised by parents in the associations it makes. It meets sights which are ill calculated to make a good impression on it. Children permitted to roam the streets at will at all hours of the night, and be the witnesses of every street fight that may occur, are certainly not receiving the best training of either their observing faculties or their moral powers. These vicious habits formed early in life are extremely difficult to eradicate. They are like weeds: the more flourishing the less the soil is tilled on which they grow.

An important question arises here as to when moral culture should begin. No doubt it is usually postponed too long. Little attention is paid to it during the earlier years of life. Nothing could be more fatal than this negligence. The child longs to be free from the treatment he receives, and he gladly hails the day which looses him from the bonds that bind him to his home. Moral nurture should begin when the physical nurture begins. There is no more important period than the first few years of the child's life. Of course the nurture must be suited to the nature of the child. We must not expect to subject it during the first year of its existence to the same moral treatment that we would in the future, any more than we would subject it to a diet suited only to the wants of an adult. The method of culture must be suited to infancy, and this must be followed by such culture as is appropriate to the successive stages of bodily development. We cannot tell the precise time at which the age of responsibility begins in any child. But we must not suppose that previous to its period of responsibility there may be no moral training. As well might we suppose that the body does not grow during this time. There is much to be done from the first day of the child's existence throughout its whole period of infancy. It is altogether a mistake to conclude that because a child cannot talk, there can therefore be no impression made on its moral nature. This is in reality the age at which the moral principles and moral character of the parent can be most effectively impressed on the child's mind. The whole life of the child is at this stage one of impressions. There is not a motion made in its presence that does not make an impression for weal or woe on its future. Every note of praise, or joy, or love, or pity — every discordant outbreak of temper or other mischievous indiscretion, is but so much proper or improper training of the heart of the child. As the parents mould this life then by their own outward acts and expressions of countenance, so will it be developed in the future, either to the glory of God or to the service of Mammon.

Admitting then that the proper moral culture begins at the first moment of the child's existence, what shall we say of the parental mode of conducting this culture? Is it always right? Is it usually right? Is the parental example what it should be? What good can come of the gossiping we so often hear at home firesides, and in what harm may it not result in the culture of the children who surround that hearth? What good can come from angrily punishing a child that is already punished by having its finger crushed or its face cut? What shall be said of those women who permit the whole culture of their children to be placed in the hands of ignorant and vicious servants? They revolt at the idea of permitting their children to attend the same school and recite in the same classes as the poor hod-carrier's ragged children, and yet they will allow this same hod-carrier's daughter to act not only as the daily nurse but also as the moral guide of their little ones at the age at which impressions for good or evil are most easily made for life. Thus day after day the moral character of the child is being formed under the most adverse circumstances. Whether the vicious example, however, be set by the parent or by the servant is a matter of little moment; it is equally pernicious whether by servant or mistress. Have you, reader, never seen a child whipped or scolded for fretfulness, when at the time the person who inflicted the punishment did not stop to inquire into the cause of this fretfulness? How often children are punished for being unwell! Don't start; it is true. Unless a child has been spoiled, in almost every instance of uneasiness or crying, there is a natural cause for it, and that cause is often sickness. Beware what sort of example you set for your children, and let me urge you never to intrust the moral training of them in the hands of any one in whose moral character and good example you have not the most unbounded confidence. It is unwomanly and unmotherly for any one to congratulate herself that her children do not give her trouble because the servants have them in sole charge. If it be necessary even for a time to place children in the care of a servant, the most scrutinizing inquiry should be made into that servant's manners, language, and character; for none of us, it is hoped, would willingly see our children grow up in the sentiments of a vicious nurse.

If there is one thing above others, it seems to me, which is well calculated to make a child hate Christianity, it is what might be called a sanctimonious or over-saintly air. It seems to the child to be contrary to all that is bright and cheerful in life, and it regards it rightly so. God has not created man that he shall not, when in a joyous mood, wear a joyous and cheerful countenance. Many, it must be admitted, believe themselves performing their highest duty to God when they wear a solemn, sober face, and tread with a sanctimonious air that distinguishes them from common men. Could anything be more ill-fitted to attract the child to embrace religion? If such were the result of all true religious experience, it were no wonder that our church-pews are often empty. May this not, after all, have something to do with the fact that so many still remain out of the church? It sometimes happens that ministers' and deacons' sons grow up to be the fastest of youth when out of reach of home influences; and this fact has been cited by those who have not embraced religion, as an argument against it. I believe that in every such case the moral and religious training at home, though well meant and conscientious, has been most sadly mistaken. What wonder that a young man dislikes religion, when everything he knows in connection with it is in direct opposition to the inner promptings of his heart? Must he believe that the devil is instigating him to be glad, cheerful, and joyous, when he should be morose, solemn, and melancholy? If this is the influence of piety, to shut out all that is bright, cheerful, and glad in this life, no wonder he abandons it, and when he escapes parental control gives full sway to his feelings. Don't let your home or your school-room be a gloomy and solemn place. Cheer it up. Show by your own life and manner and by your conversation that your hope in Christ's atoning power is unbounded, and that you are in truth happy, and you may then hope to train up your children to enjoy the same blessed happiness which shines out from your countenance and makes itself manifest in your daily life.

Another very prevalent way of discouraging piety is

in being over-exacting in manner. The love of praise is inherent in our nature, and childhood is no exception. Little children are disappointed when they do not receive that approval which is their due. How is it with the duty of parents in this matter? One mother, supposing that children are always apt to do too little, is never pleased with what her child does, at least she never manifests that pleasure. She seems to think it a duty that she should exact more from the child than it performs, lest it become loose and careless in its performance of duty. Another, looking on the more cheerful side of the picture, smiles on the child that performs its duty, and thus encourages it to continue in its course. Though the child may by no means be perfect nor fulfil its whole duty, it still receives the encouraging smile of approval or the expressed pleasure of the parent for its good acts so far as its efforts are in the right direction. No better test in this matter can be applied than for the parent to suppose himself in the place of the child for the moment. Does he look up to God, hoping for His approval of the good work he is doing? or does he suppose that inasmuch as he cannot become perfect in good, even that which he has done shall receive no credit? God smiles upon our efforts to do good, however imperfect these may be. Let the parent and teacher learn from this to imitate the glorious example set him. Give children encouragement always for well-doing, and specially in their efforts to do good; and when they obey the spirit of a law and make efforts thereby to obey the letter also, give them the approbation which is their due.

We sometimes fail to place the proper models before children. Our own example will do much always to inspire them to do right. Of course this example must be correct. And not alone is this necessary so far as right and wrong come into the question, but it must be such also as will tend to win children to the cause of Christ. Do we go around solemn, sober, and long-faced, which is itself a discouragement to the child, as being opposed to all its feelings and pleasures, we have already done much to prevent it from embracing the doctrines we hold. But the fault does not lie here alone. We place before our child imaginary models for imitation which seem little less than perfection. Our writers of story-books put before them for imitation such children as never lived, and find them before long so good that they translate them to a higher sphere. It is a noteworthy fact, if we are to credit these writers of story-books, that almost all the good boys and girls die at a very early age. Certainly this is not presenting very great inducements to the little folks to be good. But then every virtue with which we hope to find men endowed is pictured with such a halo of glory around it in the models, that the child at once loses all hopes of ever becoming what its parents would like to have it. Thus the story of Washington and his hatchet has found its way to every fireside. This is all well enough so far as it goes, but then it does n't tell the whole truth ; and the little child is made to believe the hero as perfect as Christ himself, not in this story alone, but in almost every one where the biography is written by a friend of the hero. Thus almost every man that has risen to any degree of eminence is made a hero, and his boyhood has been represented as being almost angelic. Let me say here, that however gratifying this may be to the family relatives and personal friends of the man or woman whose deeds are thus recorded, it is a very unfortunate thing for the children who are called upon to read these biographies. It discourages them. They know nothing in their own life which indicates from analogy that they are to become great or even good men, and they make no further efforts. Aiming at the sun is well enough to learn to shoot high, but then we rarely hit anything by shooting in that direction. Far better were it to take some object within range and make an effort to reach it. Don't discourage the child by placing before it such models as it cannot imitate. Don't let it think that what it may have done in the past will prevent its accomplishing anything in the future.

There are those among parents who are one thing before their children and quite another when not in their presence. They are prudential but not prudent. All their manners and movements take on an air of policy. Like the apples of the Dead Sea, outwardly they are fair enough, but they are filled with ashes. They adopt principles, and act in accordance with them because prudence and policy dictate such a course. Their piety is too much a pretence. Do they nurse the idea that their children do not see all this? They are sadly mistaken However much they may attempt to cover up their tracks, they will be discovered. What must be the influence of such action and such pretence on the mind of a yet innocent child? What must be the influence of this petty deception on the parents themselves? Do they hope to preach one thing and practice another? Do they hope to instil precepts to which their own false life in private gives the lie? It can't be done; and it is no wonder that children brought up under such influences, fair on the outside, turn out badly.

Religious life and play are not at enmity, and that piety which sets its face against play will fail to produce good results. A child begins to show evidence of its love to God, but at the same time eagerly engages in play, and sometimes even rushes from devotional services to engage in some trial of skill or wild whoop and halloo. Are we to take it for granted that the child has really no love for God, and silence this play-life and glee which bursts forth in spite of our restraint? By no means. Put the question to yourself, fond parent. Do you never, while the sermon is being preached or the hymn sung, permit your thoughts to wander from the proper channel and back to your business? Do you never hurry off to your counting-room or your business as soon as the prayer-meeting or morning worship is over? Is this to be taken as evidence that you feel no interest in your own religious welfare? Are you willing to be measured by the same rule that you apply to the child? There may be a reason for all this, but it is n't because there is no love there. Such treatment as would have the child believe that because he loves play he therefore does not love God truly, only tends to discourage him, and this discouragement in the end settles into aversion.

Let it not be understood that no restrictions are to be placed on the child. To permit children, as is frequently the case, to roam at will on the streets in the evening is, I have said, one of the surest ways of ruining them. As a part of their moral culture therefore it is necessary that the parents, and particularly the mother, make an effort to render the home so attractive and so pleasant that the children will have no desire to be on the street. Here is a fine field for the mother to exercise her taste and enforce her moral character. She can devise plays, enliven the family-circle with music, furnish pictures and books, or relate little moral stories, all of which, with much more, will render home attractive and keep the child from the temptations which beset it while on the street. What a beautiful sight it is to see a mother thus engaged in making the home glad and the hearts of her children light with her cheerful voice, which, to the little ones who almost idolize her, is the sweetest and most beautiful of earthly music! Such a mother makes a happy home, and wins the smiles of Heaven upon her work. Is n't the prize worth the getting?

While speaking of restrictions, let me refer to the Christian Sabbath. On few questions do men of religion differ so much as on the manner in which we should spend the Sabbath. It is not my purpose here to discuss this question at length. I do not propose to argue against either that school which holds this day to be one of pure religious devotion, nor against that other which regards the day as one of pure bodily rest and physical and social pleasures and recreation. It is my province here to discuss this question only so far as it concerns the moral culture of children.

How far children should be free and how far restricted on Sunday are questions of serious import and not easily answered. Many, I know, shirk the question by allowing children to spend the day as they please. With these the idea seems to be that on the Sabbath, as at other times, the sooner the children are sent to the fields or the school — and to some the difference is inappreciable — the more comfort there will be for those at home. This, if it can be called benevolence at all, is unchristian benevolence. Parents could take no surer plan of causing the child to form loose habits, while at the same time they themselves become careless and disinterested in religious matters. On the other hand, many Christian parents are apt to restrict their children too much on the Sabbath. All mirth or exuberance of feeling is checked, as if God did not love a merry heart on the Sabbath as well as at other times. Notice one of this over-strict class of parents in the treatment of his child. On Sunday it is taken to church and made to sit there with folded hands listening to the sermon but comprehending not a word. Not a movement is it permitted to make which would indicate that it is not giving the profoundest attention, nor are its eyes permitted to wander from the pulpit for a moment. When church is out, the child is taken home, where it is either put to the catechism or made to sit quietly in the house, and thus the same rigid course of treatment is continued through the day. What can we expect from this sort of treatment? Do we hope to have it long for a return of the day? It would be unreasonable to expect this. How gladly it welcomes Monday! It begins to think this the pleasantest day of the week, because it is relieved of the unnatural treatment to which it has been subjected during Sunday. It is led to look upon Sunday not specially as a day of rest, but as a day of solemnity, as a day opposed to mirth and cheerfulness. The parent who subjects his children to treatment of this kind, (and there are many of them,) though it be done under the best of intentions, is not doing for his child what he might. His treatment drives it to rebellion against religion, and is the surest way to make it hate the devotional exercises of the Sabbath.

If the austere treatment of the child is well calculated to make it hate religious services, there can, on the other hand, nothing better be said of that plan which permits children to do as they please. This is the opposite extreme, and it is no less injurious and harmful to the child's moral character than is the other. Parents who permit bird-nesting and ball-playing, or fishing, together with other sports of the same kind, to be carried on by their children on Sunday, need expect but little love for religion from those children. Of course they will love the Sabbath and hail its return joyously, because it relieves them of all work, and there will be no interruption in their plays. But the gradation from one sinful act to another is so easy and so slight that they almost involuntarily slide from one to another until they become confirmed Sabbath-breakers, however innocent their beginning, and too often turn out to be wicked men.

Both methods spoken of being objectionable, there remains yet a middle ground which is the safe one. Neither of the two preceding is the Scripture method. First, the child must feel the force of the command, "Remember the Sabbath day, to keep it holy." He must feel that here as elsewhere he is governed by a divine law which he dares neither ignore nor question, and that though an action may not in itself be positively wrong, it is nevertheless wrong as being done on the Sabbath. The child must therefore feel that there are restrictions placed on his actions and conduct for the day which do not rest on him during the other days of the week, but at the same time he can and should be made to feel that the day, even with the restrictions, is a cause for thanksgiving and joy. So much may be done to interest the child that even the restrictions are forgotten, and he learns to be grateful that this day too can be numbered among his pleasures and enjoyments.

Much will suggest itself to the mind of the thoughtful man in regard to the manner of spending this day. The Bible is filled with little stories, such as those of Joseph, Moses, Elisha, and others, which, when translated into child-language, that is such as the child can fully comprehend, never fail to interest little children. So too there are numerous pictures to be had which illustrate some part of scriptural history. How much there is in the past and the present condition of the Holy Land, in the manners and customs of its inhabitants, in everything connected with it, that is well calculated to interest not only the child but even the adult! For those who possess that invaluable gift, ability to sing, how many little Sunday-school hymns are well calculated not only to make the child bright and cheerful, but at the same time create in him an abiding love for the Saviour! It does one's heart good to hear a group of little folks join in one of these soul-stirring hymns; and how much more they enjoy them when father and mother unite with them in singing praises to God! Much can be done to entertain the child by talking to him of Christ, and presenting to the young mind the Saviour as he is, and not as a frightful and disagreeable being. Thus very much can be done to make the child's Sabbath a pleasant one. Children reared under such influences cannot fail to grow up respecting and loving the Lord's day.

Parents and teachers are engaged in no more important work, nor have they a more difficult task than the moral culture of their children. Let us hope that more thought will be paid to it in the future, and pray that our efforts at proper training may not be fruitless. We must enter on this work with a prayerful spirit. It were folly to suppose that we can accomplish so good and noble a work without the powerful assistance of God.

CHAPTER XVII.

PHYSICAL NURTURE.

THE assertion that our age is a utilitarian one has become almost trite, and we would fain deny it; but a glance at our method of doing things shows the truthfulness of it. How true it is that we are utilitarian, and yet how true it is too that we fail to accomplish much of what we aim at! While the great aim of life in a measure seems to be the accumulation of wealth, we forget that there is a certain preparation necessary in order that we may gain the end we seek. Thus while we diligently discuss the best methods of rearing stock, of training horses, and of building barns, we show our interest in these in a monetary point of view. We are anxious to discover the best breed and the most effective means of rearing sound, healthy animals. We feel the importance of surrounding our stock with such conditions as will be most conducive to their healthy development, because on this development depends their market value. All agree as to the necessity of this care for the comfort of the dumb brutes. But do we perform the same kind offices for our children? True, these receive many little attentions at our hands which the brute does not, but then are they always studied as to what results they may lead to, and are they at all times well calculated to benefit those who receive them? Certainly if it is important that our sheep, our pigs, and our cattle should have special attention that they may be developed properly, it is none the less important that the physical well-being of our children should receive still greater attention.

No one will deny the necessity of physical training that we may enjoy good health, if no other end were subserved. But this is not the only benefit wrought. We need strong bodies upon which to build our mental edifice, upon which our intellectual acquirements may be based. A sound body is no less essential than a sound mind. It needs but a glance at the professional and business men of our day to show the sad neglect of physical culture. A sound, healthy man who can stand up and declare himself free from all ills to which flesh is heir, is something of a wonder in this age. Go where we will, we hear men and women complain of some illness which unfits them in a measure for their work in the world. What a miserable, sallow-faced, long-visaged set of dyspeptics there are in this world! Almost every one we meet presents *prima-facie* evidence of some bodily ailment within. What is the cause of all this? Evidently we pay too little attention to physical culture, and, as a consequence, we are made to suffer the natural penalties resulting from our own negligence.

How to remedy this matter, and produce a race of healthy, active men and women, is a question of no little importance. Thus far the work, if any has been inaugurated, has not been productive of as much good as we might wish. Reformers have accomplished but little. Our gymnasiums have benefited a few men who have adhered to a systematic and regular course of training, but the mass of those who have gone there have taken to it kindly for a month or two and then become careless, and have therefore derived but little benefit. The mistake in our system of physical culture is, that we have commenced at the wrong end of the work. We have attempted to break up habits which have been the formation of a lifetime, and consequently have in the main failed. To make a reformation in this matter, we must begin our work in the school-room and at the home fireside; not with the adults of the family, but with the children. I believe that in this, as in other reforms, the proper starting-point is home. Parents have it just as much in their power to train, in the course of a generation or two, a healthy, well-developed set of children as they have to produce fine specimens of horses and cattle. This may seem commonplace talk, but the subject is a commonplace one and demands it. If we find that by a little attention and care we can so train our children that they shall be better able to attend to the multitudinous duties of life, and be less liable to fall into the hands of the physician or prove the victim of the apothecary, why shall we not devote some attention to doing for them at least as much as we do for our live-stock?

One of the specialties to which parents must give attention is the food of children. I have known mothers who, it seemed to me, possessed no more discretion in this matter than the infants they held in their arms.

They allowed their children, even the smallest, to eat everything that came within reach, from a crab-apple to a delicate morsel of sugar, and then wondered what could possibly make their little ones so restless at night, and why it was so often necessary to call in the doctor. Others, following the other extreme, have withheld everything but a special diet, on which they have trained their children almost to shadows. They are made to look very fragile and delicate, but they by no means enjoy good health. Others still there are who, from the moment of the child's waking in the morning until its going to rest at night, are continually giving it food at every demand, thus keeping the stomach in a continued state of activity, until at length its tone and power become so much impaired that the child's chances of filling a dyspeptic's grave are usually promising. Much of all this may be the result of ignorance, but doubtless much of it also arises from either negligence or a desire to silence the child. All these methods of treatment are wrong. Had I the space here I would like to say much more on this subject, but as it is I must confine myself to a few of the leading points, hoping to draw the attention of parents to the matter, if I can accomplish nothing more.

The child should not be permitted to make a gormand of itself, nor, on the other hand, should it be deprived of having all that is necessary to answer the demands of its system. Allowing it to eat too much or giving it too little would both be detrimental to health; but the latter is probably the more dangerous, as its injurious effects are the more lasting. There is little danger of a child's eating too much unless it has been deprived to some extent before of such food as it needed. It is not the animal that roams all day in the meadow that is foundered by drinking too much, but the one that has for too long a time been deprived of its supply of water. So too a child which has before it a mixed and variable diet, both vegetable and animal—for children as well as adults need some animal food to strengthen them—is not apt to become a glutton. It is the child that from day to day is compelled to subsist on the same unchangeable and therefore, in a measure, unhealthy dish. All physiologists agree on this point, that our system demands food in sufficient quantity and in variety. There is no point in which parents make a greater mistake than in withholding fruit from their children and supplying them with pastry in its stead. The true policy would be less pastry and more fruit. There is little danger in eating ripe fruit in its proper season, but there is danger in eating hot cakes and rich pies and puddings. It is not the eating of ripe fruit that gives rise to so much sickness among children during the summer months, but the eating of that which is unripe. Briefly, then, it is necessary that the food of our children should be abundant and varied, and contain such nutritive qualities as will fit it for the wants of the growing child.

A second specialty requiring the attention of parents is the dress of their children. I do not allude here to the material nor to the color or cost, but to the comfort. The tendency in all classes of society, and especially in that class particularly anxious to be fashionable, is towards a disposition to dress too scantily. Two reasons exist for this: the first, and the one generally urged, is, that it is necessary to harden children; the second, and often the real reason is that the child is supposed to look prettier in this scanty dress than when fully clad. Of the first theory it may be said, that children can, to a certain extent, be hardened, but they are those only who are hardened by constant exposure. The rustic farmer-boy who is accustomed during the whole year to spend much of his time in the open air, pays but little attention to the driving snows of winter; but the city-bred youth, whose hours are spent in the school-room or by the warm family fireside, may not venture out without proper protection on a cold winter day. The change from one temperature to the other is so sudden that he exposes himself to great danger of receiving such a shock as will forever unfit him for duty. This principle does not seem to be fully understood by parents, and, as a consequence, it may be said with truth, that the foundation for disease is laid at an early age, and the child is made to suffer during a lifetime for the ignorance or indiscretion of a foolish parent. Instead of being better able to endure extreme cold, children are really less able than adults. It is a mistaken notion that because they do not complain they are therefore not suffering. True, children who are in a healthy condition may suffer less inconvenience from the driving storms than those older whose physical nurture has been neglected; but the grown person, other things being equal, is better able than the child to endure cold. This being true, what shall be said of the style in which mothers too often dress their children during even the cold days of winter? Who of us would willingly, so far as comfort is concerned, dress in the manner we dress our children? There is no reason why we should ask them to submit to hardships and treatment which in our own experience we find detrimental to both comfort and health. It is folly for parents to clothe their little children during the colder portions of the year in such a manner as to expose a part of their body or their limbs. What with the injudicious treatment of children with regard to diet in summer and scantiness of clothing in winter, it is no wonder that the mortality among them is so great. I am averse to saying unpleasant things, but duty to my subject compels me to say that I believe parents in many cases guilty of the death of their own children through negligence. The responsibility of rearing children physically is much greater than most persons are willing to acknowledge.

There is also sometimes a difficulty arising from overdress. Parents are in their anxiety often over-cautious, and clothe their children too warm, thus making them liable to take cold when exposed to the slightest draft of air. Great caution is needed here. As a general rule, the amount of clothing should be varied according to the temperature of the atmosphere. More is necessary when we are standing or sitting still than when moving about, and more when we are in the open air than when in a room. Clothing too should be kept scrupulously neat and clean, and not only is this necessary as a part of proper physical nurture, but as a part of moral nurture as well. Don't however allow this neatness to assume that false shape which prevents the child from enjoying its share of play. If the child wear such fanciful fabrics, or so fancifully constructed, that it cannot enjoy every play suited to happy and innocent childhood, then is its dress in so far opposed to its true physical culture. Those dresses which will not permit it to run, and jump, and frolic around, with of course the usual amount of tripping and tumbling, are unsuitable. The child feels such a dress an encumbrance, and when the little fellow is called back from chasing a butterfly or scrambling up a bank, because he may soil his clothes, he heartily wishes himself divested of such clothing and allowed to enjoy himself according to his taste. This exercise is just what the child most needs when the clothing is deficient. The less clothing worn, particularly during the colder parts of the year, the greater the amount of food necessary to supply the requisite amount of animal heat. This is a truism which every intelligent farmer understands, and in the care of his stock he makes them as comfortable as possible that they may consume less food.

The desire for play is usually so great in children that little effort is necessary to secure for them the proper amount of exercise. Now and then, however, parents and teachers, under a mistaken notion of making their boys and girls appear like grown-up men and women, prohibit them from engaging in that exercise which is of all kinds most beneficial. In this case there is nothing left but to resort to something more formal in its character than unrestrained play. Exercise of some kind the child must have, otherwise its development cannot be healthy. In the rural districts, by the daily work in the fields and amid all the simplicity and beauty of nature, the rustic lad usually grows up strong and robust; but in the cities the young are in a measure denied the privilege of communing with nature, and a different development is usually the result. Nothing argues more strongly the necessity of pleasant surroundings when we exercise. Although work therefore may answer for exercise, it is only when that work is pleasant and agreeable that it does its full measure of good. Exercise of all kinds must be undertaken with a light heart and with the mind entirely abstracted from our cares and business. No one is benefited by that exercise to which he goes as a task; nor, on the other hand, can one expect good results from his exercise when his mind is entirely engaged with something else. The young student who takes a few turns up and down the gravel walk with the mind busily intent on the tasks or lessons claiming his attention, is trying to do two things at once, and does neither well. So too the young man who hastily snatches a few moments of his time and rushes to the gymnasium to have a few turns on the "Flying Dutchman" or leap once or twice over the bar, and then suddenly return to his business, might as well have spared himself the whole of his time; for the good he has gained from his exercise is little.

It is amusing to watch persons at times walking for exercise, as it is called. They mope and slouch along as if they went to their work with anything but a glad heart. Exercise of this kind is almost worthless. God has implanted in the child a desire for play which forms its substitute for any formal exercise, and we learn a valuable lesson from this play which we may apply not only in benefiting ourselves, but also in our manner of aiding the child to secure the most perfect and healthy development. It was evidently meant that we, too, should enter upon our work cheerfully and with a light heart, forgetting for a time the cares of the world. Let us interpose no obstacles to the working out of God's plan. Formal exercise is of course not without its benefits also, but in comparison with those derived from play as a strengthening and developing process, it is of little moment. This activity of body is absolutely necessary to preserve the healthy tone of the physical part of man, and upon man's physical health depends, in a great measure, the health and vigor of his mind. That system of government, then, in a family or a school, which tabooes romping and play as undignified, is not only mistaken but also mischievous. No formal system, whatever its merits, can take the place of play.

Nothing is probably more essential to health than pure air. In order that the blood may be pure, the air which purifies it must first be pure. The instances of disease arising from breathing foul air are so numerous and so common that it is unnecessary here to refer to them. But there is comparatively so little attention after all given to the ventilation of rooms that the matter cannot be brought too often or too prominently into notice. It is said that as a class the miners of England break down prematurely from bronchitis and pneumonia caused by the atmosphere in which they live. In our own mining districts it is a rare thing to find an aged man who has spent much of his life in the unhealthy air of the mines. So, too, we find that different tradesmen, being subject to the impurities of different atmospheres, usually die prematurely, according to the vicious qualities of the air they breathe. These are facts patent to every one. But there are other deaths caused and other diseases engendered in our own households that are no less alarming in their character, which do not generally receive attention. It is often a source of wonder why so many children are scrofulous. We are apt to think that it is all hereditary. This is a mistake. In the Norwood school, England, where scrofula broke out among its six hundred pupils so extensively as to carry off great numbers, Dr. Arnott was employed to investigate the cause, and immediately traced it not to insufficient food, as was at first supposed, but to "defective ventilation and consequent atmospheric impurity." A case in point occurred in one of the most prominent of our educational institutions in this country a few years ago. The air from the cess-pools, through defective drainage, circulated more or less through the building occupied by the students as dormitories, and as the natural result typhoid fever set in, and but few escaped the attack. While referring to this matter, let me say that too great caution cannot be exercised in the arrangement of buildings so as to prevent the foul air of the cess-pools from mingling with the air we

16 *

breathe, as in the great majority of cases it is the fruitful source of that disastrous fever known as typhoid.

Many diseases are propagated through the impurities of the atmosphere. Thus it is said that from the body of one afflicted with scarlet fever, a cloud of fine dust may be seen rising when it is uncovered in the sunlight. Of course this and other diseases are propagated in other ways, but the atmosphere is an effective medium, and by means of it the poisonous seeds of disease are rapidly disseminated. Cases innumerable could be cited where disease has been contracted not only in the sick-room but by breathing the impurities of the atmosphere of the living-room. Nothing will so soon develop scrofula, consumption, and other diseases of the kind, as impure air. Let us see to it then that the air of our rooms is not filled with impurities and seeds of disease. Better by far suffer the cool air which by means of ventilators finds its way into the room, and use up a little more fuel, than by keeping our doors and windows closed and chinked, pen in disease and death while we shut out the fierce but refreshing wind.

Of the morbid effects of breathing impure air, Dr. Ray says: "In a school, or hospital, or other considerable assemblage of people, the purity of the air may be pretty accurately measured by the amount of cheerfulness, activity, and lively interest which pervades it; and yet, so little do people think or care about this subject, that, under existing arrangements, there are very few who do not every day of their lives inspire more or less highly vitiated air. The listlessness and stupidity of students, and especially of children confined in the school-room, are often due to the bad state of the air they breathe. Using the brain in a vitiated atmosphere is like working with a blunted instrument, and the effect of course must be aggravated when the inexperienced are first learning the use of the instrument." Who that has ever taught has not experienced this? It isn't any wonder that pupils become dull and listless in our schools, nor that we see so many nodding heads in our church-pews on the Sabbath. Let us attend to the ventilation of our public buildings, and we shall be able to make at least a partial reformation. The supply of pure air is so great, and the harmony between the wants of animal and vegetable life so perfect, that there is no danger of exhausting the supply. On this ground therefore there is no excuse, nor can there be any on the ground of expense, as it is free to every one. Let us apply then to our school-rooms and home firesides the principles which govern its distribution. We are all right in theory and have been for some time, but we are yet sadly lacking in practice.

A point to which special attention should be directed is the amount of mental labor children are permitted to perform. In general, when left to their own choice, they are not apt to injure themselves by over-study, but there are exceptions to this rule. Children may be so influenced by both parents and teachers as to perform under certain circumstances too much brain-work. Numerous instances might be cited of a fever contracted here, a debilitated system there, the evident results of too much study and too little exercise. One pupil's attendance is irregular, another complains of almost constant headache, while still another is compelled for some months to abandon school-life. Some of this results from over-study, but there is also another cause. Parents who are constantly permitting themselves to be overtaxed with brain-work become more or less weakened in their physical functions, and transmit these same defects to their children. That the child therefore may have a healthy brain, that of the parent must also be healthfully exercised.

It is a matter of some importance what habits we permit children to contract, and this not less in their physical than in their moral nature. One of these, and one more generally neglected than most persons would be willing to acknowledge, is personal cleanliness. We have too many belonging to the "great unwashed." Evidences are so plentiful all around us that a reference to them is all that is necessary. It requires some degree of courage to enter some of our primary schools where the ventilation is defective. It is n't all foul air breathed from the lungs that makes the difference between that atmosphere and the one you so much long for out-of-doors. The exhalations rising from the bodies of those children add much to the sum of the impurities that almost drive one back as he attempts to enter. In order to health it is necessary that the perspiration which is thrown out by the sweat-glands of the skin be removed. This must be done frequently, and it is necessary to secure the proper working of these glands. Not only is it necessary that we bathe regularly, but our clothing, which takes up all the impurities thrown off by the skin, must be changed frequently and aired. Our bed-clothing also should receive an airing daily that the atmosphere may carry off the impurities with which it becomes saturated during the night. Much may be done in having children improve themselves, if a little assistance is given by older heads.

It is a rare thing to find an erect man or woman. The contracting of bad habits in sitting and standing and long continuance in them have in a great measure tended to destroy our beauty and symmetry, and now we find erect, well-formed men and women the exception. There is no doubt that this is all the result of habit. It is a rare case to find a small child stooping or round-shouldered. School-life often does much toward making children crooked, and especially is this true when the benches on which the children sit are uncomfortable on account of being too high or without comfortable resting places for the back. In both sitting and standing, children are permitted to assume positions which are neither graceful nor healthful. How seldom we find a man who does not feel extremely awkward when made to stand where he has not some means of support! To say nothing of the ungracefulness of these stooping postures, the injury of which they are the fruitful source should be sufficient to condemn them. It is utterly impossible for any one in a stooping posture to inflate his lungs to their full capacity; hence a certain amount of vitality is lost and a portion of the poison which should be eliminated from the system is retained, and the seeds of disease disseminated.

Caution should be exercised that proper habits be early formed, and that these become regular. The irregularities to which many subject not only themselves but also their children, are enough to sap the vitality of any one's system. Breakfast this morning at six, to-morrow at eight, and next day at seven, is enough to make any one's stomach rebel and become dyspeptic. Yet how many families there are in which the meals are subject to as much irregularity as this, with an occasional lunch just before retiring thrown in! In the matter of sleep, too, the same may be said. One evening the child is required to retire with the fading out of twilight, and the next it remains awake until probably ten or later. Thus the habit becomes irregular, and sleep is robbed of half of its beneficial influence. As to the amount of sleep necessary, no definite rule can be given. It is modified by the physical and mental condition of the person, and differs as much in its requirements as does the quantity of food. As a general rule, however, no one should be waked as long as he is sleeping soundly. It is little less than cruel to rouse a child in the morning from sound sleep. Nature in this is a safer guide than vacillating man.

The physical nurture of children is a matter of some importance, and it is necessary that parents in assuming the responsibility, and they alone must assume it, should be prepared for the work. If they understand the secrets of preventing disease, it is worth to them more than all the cures from yarrow-tea down to the most insignificant that sage old grandames may urge. The results of parental negligence and parental ignorance in this matter are almost beyond conception. There are both an over-care and an under-care of which parents are guilty, and either is in many cases fatal to long life and happiness. It is not right that we should train up a child as we would cultivate a green-house plant, shutting it away from the joys and feelings to be experienced only in the open air; nor is it, on the other hand, right to train it up as we would a colt from which we expect nothing that is good, turning it out into storms and sunshine alike, or shutting it in a close apartment, where, with every breath it draws, it inhales also deadly poison. Ignorance and negligence, when so much opportunity exists for enlightenment, is criminal.

I have often felt that our course of school studies might be improved by the introduction of physiology. I would not have it usurp the place of any other study now in the course, although there are those which are of far less importance, but it should either be added or be granted a portion of the time devoted now to other branches. It is important that every parent should understand physiology and hygiene, and it is of the utmost importance that every teacher be acquainted with the subject, so that if the study cannot be adopted as one of the regular course, the teacher may still convey the most valuable part of it by means of informal lectures or talks. The teacher who talks to his pupils on these points will always have an attentive audience. It is to be hoped that our efforts at physical nurture will not all rest in words, but that some active work will be performed, and that parents and teachers will enlighten themselves, and earnestly add their efforts in assisting to develop a more healthy and more perfect race.

CHAPTER XVIII.

TOO EARLY AT SCHOOL.

ONE of the wisest changes the Legislature of Pennsylvania ever made in her school law is that which prohibits children from entering the public schools before the age of six instead of five, as the law stood previously, and there is probably no law on their statute-book which has been the source of more grumbling on the part of unthinking, ignorant parents. I have referred before to the mistake of sending children to school too young, and I shall give additional reasons why the mistake should not be tolerated. Some may differ from me on this point, yet from all the arguments ever urged, I am still more fully convinced that sending children to school, as schools are usually conducted, before the age of six, is a serious mistake.

There is much knowledge that children gain independent of what they acquire in school. From the moment that light first seems to break through into the mind of the child, its life is a continuous course of acquiring knowledge. Not an object escapes its attention. The flowers of the garden, the grass of the fields, the pebbles at the brookside, the variegated foliage of the trees, the machinery on the farm — everything claims its notice. Is not all the knowledge that it gains in this way valuable? How much better would it be doing in school learning the letters of the alphabet at the rate of one a week, or even one a day! It seems to me that this communing with nature is of infinitely more importance in the earlier years of life than the knowledge the child usually acquires.

Let me call your attention to a familiar scene. On a hillside stands a country school-house. Ranged around the interior are little benches, some with backs and some without. Some of these are so high that the children are compelled to sit on them without being able to touch the floor. As a consequence the position they are made to assume is unhealthful, and their spines become more or less curved. You find your own child of five or six years among these, and he is enjoying himself much as the rest. When requested to study, their eyes are directed to books, but what can they study? What could you and I study with the same previous mental training, if a set of arbitrary characters were placed before us without our knowing what future use we should be able to make of them? We would count it but folly if asked to study them. Much less do the children find in them anything to study. When the teacher no longer keeps his eye on them, they engage themselves as they think best, and now and then throw a paper wad at a neighbor, spit at some one's toes as a target, or amuse themselves in one of the other ways known only to schoolboys. This in general makes up the sum of their enjoyments. Of course in many well-regulated schools they are furnished with little slates and amuse themselves with these, but in this school we find, on inquiry, that the parents don't see the use of slates, and hence refuse to purchase any for their children. We might enter more into detail and sketch the more minute parts of the picture, but want of space forbids. What good is your child doing in this place? Is it learning rapidly? Is its physical system being strengthened by the impure air and lack of vigorous exercise? Are its moral faculties being strengthened by the deception it is taught to practise when required to do that which is impossible? If none of these, you must agree with me that it were better at home, revelling in sunlight and pure air, gleaning such knowledge as nature designs it should at this age.

Another difficulty presents itself just here. The child that begins school-life too early becomes in the course of a year or two tired of the confinement which imprisons it. There is nothing in the school that seems to be pleasant and in harmony with the inquisitiveness and play instincts of the child. Day after day it is made to go through the same drill and tread the same plank, and by the time it is prepared to understand the school-work and the objects of school-going, it has become so thoroughly tired and disgusted that insuperable obstacles are already placed in the way of its advancement. I am convinced that there is but little accomplished by sending children to school so long before they know the object in being sent. But little difference can be noticed at the age of nine in the advancement of those who began at five and those who began at seven. The progress of the one has been slow and tedious, while that of the other has been pleasant and rapid. The latter is in reality in most cases the better fitted of the two for continuing the work, because the general knowledge he has acquired previous to his school-days is such that it renders him great assistance, and his faculties are besides bright and active.

An objection to which I have before referred is the length of time small pupils are required to remain in the school-room. They find but little pleasure in remaining thus imprisoned six hours of the day. My own little boy, when asking him a few days ago whether he would like to go to school, put in this plea without, so far as I know, ever having heard any one say anything about it: "Papa, they stay in too long. I would rather be at home and say my lessons here." I felt that though it was but the argument of a child, he understood the question better and was nearer the philosophy of it than many an older head. They do stay in too long, and that very fact is a strong argument against sending children to school very young.

Were our schools conducted according to the Pestalozzian system or after the kindergarten method of Germany, some of the objections would be of no force. Our homes, however, come much nearer the kindergarten idea than primary schools do. Children at home usually are allowed to exercise their observing faculties to a great extent, and are at the same time permitted to play much in the open air, being confined to the house but little, so that their mental and their physical development, together with the moral, are more healthy.

Why, it may be asked, are parents so anxious to have their children enter school early? Do they expect them to learn rapidly? Do they expect by this forced culture to strengthen mind and body? Not so, I fear. It is a question which I do not like to answer for any one, but were I to give my own opinion, I should have to say that I believe in many cases parents are anxious to have their children out of the way at home. I don't like benevolence of this kind. It smacks too much of self-interest at the expense of the well-being of the child which is yet too young and too weak to enter its protest. If it be the result of parental ignorance, let us by all means strive to enlighten parents as to their duty. If it be from the selfish motives to which I have alluded, that parents may enjoy more comfort at home, it is the duty of every one of us to set his face against it and try to break it down. We cannot justify the practice in either case.

Really the little amount of good accomplished by our smallest pupils, those under the age of six or seven, is of so small moment that it can certainly present no inducement to send the child for that purpose. Of course there may be exceptions to this, and I suppose, my dear reader, that your child possibly forms one of these exceptions; possibly not, but I am sure that fifteen minutes a day devoted to instruction at home by the mother or the father will accomplish vastly more good, and the child will love the acquisition of learning under such tuition. If parents will go to the expense of furnishing the child with a slate and a few simple playthings, it will cause them but little trouble and be but little in their way. Its school-days under such circumstances will be remembered with pleasure. Is it not worth the effort? Can teachers do nothing towards showing parents their way clear in this matter? I know it is not a pleasant duty, as our motives may be misjudged, but it is certainly worth a trial.

CHAPTER XIX.

TRAINING FOR LIFE'S DUTIES.

I WOULD not have it understood, as might be inferred from the topic here discussed, that the preparation of the child for the active duties of life is the only or even the main preparation necessary. I have in a preceding chapter had occasion to refer to this subject, in which I at the time attempted to make clear my idea of the end of all education. It were folly, however, to argue that an active preparation for the duties of this life is not also necessary. Men and women who give no attention to the world in which they are placed, it seems to me, put a slight estimate on the omniscience of the God who created them and placed them in this preparatory school, to say nothing of their lack of capacity and fitness as guides to the rest of mankind.

All young men in a country like ours, where there is no national social distinction, where the ploughboy and the son of the millionaire sit on the same bench at school, recite in the same class, and compete in the same contest for either prize or power, expect to enter some business in life. They expect to be either tradesmen, farmers, mechanics, or professional men. In short they expect to be business men in the most comprehensive sense of the term. The great question for us to solve is, shall they be prepared for the active duties they will be called upon to perform, or shall they, like most of our own generation, be allowed to strike out for themselves in life without a guiding hand to steer and direct them on even their first perilous voyage? If the latter, it will not be surprising to find them, like wrecked ships, thrown upon the rocks and dashed to pieces for the want of a skilful pilot, and proper instructions to guide them; nay, it is surprising that so many under the circumstances do succeed.

An important qualification which many men in all vocations lack, is the ability to read human nature; and yet there is scarcely a calling in life which does not require a keen insight into human nature. Possibly nothing so much determines the success of professional men — preachers, teachers, doctors, and lawyers — as shrewdness in judging human nature; and yet how few there are comparatively who are well skilled in this subtle art! How few preachers there are who talk directly to their congregations, attacking the devil and his minions in just the spot most vulnerable! How few make it a business to study men in their daily occupations, the merchant behind his counter, the mechanic in his shop, or the farmer at his plow! We have a few, it is true, who seem to understand this secret of success, and their works have been bountifully blessed in the conversion of souls, but there are still too few. Too many are still satisfied, not only in this but also in other professions, to follow in the footsteps of their predecessors. It is necessary also that the teacher be a keen judge of human nature, as no one has to deal with its subtleties more than he. Not only is it necessary for his own welfare, but also that he may train those under his care for the general duties incumbent upon them.

How little training do children receive for the positions they will be called upon to assume in society! Little civilities and politenesses which make up much of the sum of social life seem to attract little special attention; and yet how important they are! Every modest young man knows how unpleasant a thing it is to go into society when he understands nothing of what will be expected of him. In towns where there are frequent social evening gatherings this is not so much the case, but there is a sad neglect of social training in the country. The teacher in his school-room and the parent in the family can do much towards improving the condition of things, and we certainly need it.

There are home duties which will be required of our boys and girls as they grow up to be men and women, which should not be neglected. The mother whose daughter sits idle while she toils and hurries herself to her grave, is, to say the least, an unfortunate if not a very foolish woman. If it be the daughter's fault, then is the mother unfortunate; if her own, then foolish. It is high time that this silly twaddle of young ladies, that they were not brought up to work, were done away with. The mischief that has been wrought by it is incalculable. The silly young girl who can ring out a merry laugh and declare that she knows nothing of baking and cooking, that her mother or the girl does all such work, is a very unfortunate young woman, and there are few sensible young men who would care to have such for a wife. I am aware that this is plain talk, but I think I understand how worthy young men think on this matter. If there is one point above others on which a mother should pride herself on the accomplishments of her daughter, it seems to me it is not her music, not her painting, not her dancing, not her ability to write poetry, but her qualifications in the matter of household management and making a happy and cheerful home. Mothers can do nothing which will prove more beneficial to the future welfare and happiness of their daughters and their daughters' homes than giving them such training and instruction as will best fit them for the duties they will be called upon to assume in gracing homes of their own and rendering them cheerful, pleasant, and happy. This is of infinitely more value than all the lessons they may take in painting and drawing or in fancy and ornamental work during their school course. I am aware that this smacks of utilitarianism, but even the narrowest and most contracted utilitarianism is less objectionable than wild and visionary theory which melts at the most delicate touch of practical common sense.

The young need special training for the duties they will have to perform as citizens. Too little attention has been paid to this in the past. Evidences of it are painfully prevalent everywhere. It is a rare case indeed that a man is selected to fill an office because of his special fitness for it. But there are duties independent of those falling to the lot of public officials, which should be understood by all those who will be called upon in the future to participate in conducting the public affairs of the country. We need intelligent voters that the life of the government may not be endangered by the ballots of men who know not what they are voting for. We need honest and good men who will enter the political arena that base, grovelling politicians may not, under the plea of patriotism, let out the life-blood of the nation. We need everywhere men who understand the principles upon which our government is founded, and who are willing and honest enough to support those principles though it may be detrimental to the interests of their own political party. We need among our public men such as understand at least so much of the principles underlying our government that they need not necessarily be dependent entirely upon their clerks for the requisite knowledge to perform properly the duties of offices to which they have been called. Mark here that the introduction of partisan politics into the school is by no means advocated, but instead that broad, general training which teaches men their duty to their government, which fits them for exercising the right of suffrage, which makes them broad-minded, generous politicians and good citizens. There is nothing partisan in this kind of training, and the man who makes it such deserves the lash of public criticism and public censure.

Our youth, to fit them for their duties as citizens, should be trained in sentiments of patriotism. There should be developed in their hearts a love for our own country and her institutions. They should be taught to feel that an insult offered to her is an insult to every one of her children. They should be made to feel that they are specially interested in preserving her honor and protecting her rights. Much should be made of those holidays which celebrate some event in her history. We have become too cool in our celebration of such memorable events as the Signing of the Declaration of Independence. Business, money-making, Mammon, has almost crowded out the day. This is all wrong. Let us revive the memory of these days and all others that tend to beget in our children that pride in our government which ever acts as the bulwark of the nation's liberty. Let the days of '76 not be forgotten by our boys and girls. Let us make our hearts young again by entering with them into the celebration of these days with our old enthusiasm, and we shall be able to inspire in them a love for our country which shall ever be her surest safeguard in time of danger.

CHAPTER XX.

UNIVERSAL EDUCATION NECESSARY.

IT is well known that in most of the States of our Union a public or free-school system exists. We pride ourselves on the advantages offered by these schools to children of all classes. They have been the boast of our eloquent orators ever since they were called into existence. Our historians have never failed to call attention to this feature of our government; and yet, with all, it may be questioned whether we have not overrated our educational standing as a nation.

In countries in which free schools do not exist, education is to a great extent the privilege of the wealthy few. Money alone purchases it, and of course those not possessing the necessary means must remain uneducated. Examples are plentiful all around us among those of the subjects of royalty who have sought an asylum in our republic. True, there are a few monarchies which lay special stress on the education of their citizens; but they are very few. Yet I think sometimes that we are inclined to praise our own country too highly and give others too little credit. In China, for instance, a country which we have been accustomed to regard as one of the lowest educationally, liberal culture, especially in literature, is made a part of the necessary preparation for holding office. It is said that the cultivation of literature is professedly the only channel of introduction to advancement in the State and to the acquisition of office, rank, and honors. Necessarily the number of students becomes great, and a taste for letters is almost universally diffused. Schools are found in every village, and the best education may be procured on the most moderate terms. Public examinations are held twice a year and presents are distributed to the most deserving. A grand national college named *Han-lin-yen* is located at Pekin. It is supported by the government, and its members consist of the chief literati of the empire. Works on literary history, criticism, and biography are numerous. M. Abel-Remusat says: "There is not a nation, even in Europe, that has so many books, books so well made, so commodious for consultation, and at so low a price." Their imperial geography alone forms 260 volumes in quarto, with maps and plans. Among the topics embraced in it are topography, hydrography, monuments, antiquities, natural curiosities, industry, commerce, agriculture, productions, government, general history, biography, and bibliography. Real science and literature are, however, at a low ebb, because nothing but the old-established principles are taught. But, after all, is not their example a good one in requiring culture before intrusting in the hands of the applicant the office he seeks? It is an interesting question and worthy at least some consideration. It needs no argument with those who understand the way in which our public offices are filled, nor with those who have measured the capacity of our office-holders, to show that our condition is susceptible of improvement.

I have not the space nor do I wish to enter into a prolonged discussion of this question here, but there are many arguments which might be cited to show the desirableness, if not the necessity, of universal education on the grounds of good citizenship alone. Our government is of course better than the Chinese, in that it is republican, offering the same facilities nominally to rich and poor; and for this very reason we should insist the more strenuously on the education of all our citizens. We know not who among us may be called to fill positions of honor or trust. It may fall to your lot or mine; it may fall to the lot of the most humble individual among us. The distribution of public offices is peculiarly uncertain. It were better that merit and fitness should always govern in the selection of officers; but since they do not, let us have all prepared to assume the duties of such offices as they may be called upon to fill. Let us at least feel that all who are entitled to the ballot according to the requirements of our government, are prepared to vote understandingly. If there are voters now who are led to the polls as oxen to the slaughter, it is so much the more necessary that those whom we are training to control the affairs of government hereafter, be educated, not one-tenth nor one-half of them, but all. It will not mend matters for political parties to cry "Fraud!" to each other; the mistake lies to a great extent in the misdirected and imperfect education of the past, and it is for the sober, thoughtful parents and teachers of the present generation to avoid this mistake in the future.

However much we may boast of our free schools and the good they have done, it is certain that education is by no means universal. Now, how can we remedy the defects? Can it be done by compulsory attendance? Whatever the arguments in favor of compulsory attendance, it is doubtful whether it could lay claims to making education universal, although it might do much towards bringing about such a result. Can it be done by making education the basis of suffrage? There is no doubt that this would have great force. Of course there are grave objections arising which would make it inexpedient to put a measure of this kind in force suddenly. It were better to adopt it with the proviso, that after a specified time the law shall go into operation. In this way none of those who now enjoy the right of suffrage would be deprived of any of their privileges. Thus, establishing an educational basis for suffrage, it is believed that all American citizens and those desirous of becoming such would educate not only themselves but also their children. It would operate in this country much as the Chinese requirement of literary culture in public officers, by securing the education of the masses. I throw out the thought for the consideration of my readers, and I ask them to give it some attention. It is a question which affects the welfare of the whole republic, and on it in a great measure depends the stability of our government.

It is not long since it was thought unnecessary to educate girls. Indeed there are sections of our own State to-day, and I suppose the same is true of other States, where this idea still prevails to some extent. A knowledge of household duties and such work as falls to the lot of women on our farms is frequently held to be all that is necessary. The dweller in the city or other region where this notion does not prevail may doubt this; but it is true, as the statistics of the schools in the sections referred to prove. The average attendance compared with that of boys is often not greater than one-fourth. It is a lamentable fact that such notions prevail among parents in many sections even at this late day.

Miss Davies, in speaking of the education of girls, aptly says: "*Some* education is held to be indispensable, but how much is an open question; and the general indifference operates in the way of continually postponing it to other claims, and, above all, in shortening the time allotted to systematic instruction and discipline. Parents are ready to make sacrifices to secure a tolerably good and complete education for their sons; they do not consider it necessary to do the same for their daughters. Or perhaps it would be putting it more fairly to say that a very brief and attenuated course of instruction, beginning late and ending early, is believed to constitute a good and complete education for a woman.

"A very usual course seems to be for girls to spend their early years in a hap-hazard kind of way, either at home or in not very regular attendance at an inferior school, after which they are sent for a year or two to a school or college to finish. The heads of schools complain with one voice that they are called upon to 'finish' what has never been begun, and that to attempt to give anything like a sound education in the short time at their disposal, is perfectly hopeless." Although these remarks were made by an English lady with special reference to English girls, they will apply equally well to the case of American girls.

As regards the special education of girls, I refer the reader to Richter's "Levana." Let me present here another extract from that excellent work: "The education of daughters," says the author, "is the first and most important business of mothers, because it may be uninterrupted, and continue till the daughter's hand glides straight from the mother's into that which holds the wedding-ring. The boy is educated by a many-toned world, school-classes, universities, travels, business, and libraries; the mother's mind educates the daughter."

No one is a fitter teacher of the child than the mother. Primary schools, as generally conducted, are a sort of necessary evil. Home is the best school and the mother the best teacher. It is only because so many mothers are incompetent or have not the time to attend to their own children that schools for smaller pupils have been established. Were education universal, so that all mothers would prove competent to train their own children, we could dispense to a great extent with primary grades of schools, unless indeed the mother were engaged in such employment as would prevent her being the guide and instructor of her own children.

This brings up an important question: Is a lady morally justifiable in following such a business or profession as prevents her assuming the place which God in His wisdom has assigned her as the moral and intellectual guide and protector of her own offspring? I am aware that I am touching on a question which seems to oppose the doctrines so plausibly argued by some female lecturers of the day, but it is a question of common sense and a question of duty to our offspring and to God. I am willing that the reader shall answer this question for himself or herself, as the case may be, but I don't want it considered on exceptional cases. Let it be considered on the basis on which an omniscient God has founded all human society, and not on that false one which a grumbling and discontented few would establish for us. Let it be considered on the only ground sanctioned by nature and religion, in which the husband is the head of the family, as God meant he should be, and then apply the argument of common sense, and not ridicule, and we are prepared to answer the question intelligently.

Our education of women has thus far been too much restricted. It is doubtful if a more important work exists than that falling to the lot of the mother in training up her children aright. The mother, as the regulator of home affairs, the minister to the sick, the moral and religious guide to her husband, and children, and servants, fills an office more important and more sacred than all the trades, and occupations, and professions combined. Let her not therefore covet positions which nature may never have designed her to fill. She can have no more honorable and holy office than the one she now graces and ever has graced since the creation. Although I speak as a man, I know there are few sensible women who do not fully agree with me on this question.

If my position is correct, then are all our systems of education more or less defective, because the fundamental principles necessary to be taught are either omitted, or are the privilege of the few. Much of the knowledge which should be possessed by every mother and every teacher can be acquired only in private institutions from which the poor are to a great extent debarred. Should we not therefore make these privileges universal by offering as great facilities in every respect to acquire a substantial practical education in our public schools as can be given in private institutions? It can be done. More money will be required to pay better qualified teachers, that those who enter the profession may have sufficient inducement to make the necessary preparation to discharge their duties faithfully and properly; and here is where the greatest difficulty lies. Money is, after all, a greater object with many men than the welfare of their families. Let the moral guidance and the intellectual training of the young once become the most important items in the estimation of parénts, and we shall have little to fear.

If education is necessary for a man in order to be successful in business, why should it be less necessary for a woman, when her work is fully as important? And if it is necessary that the education of boys be substantial and practical in order to prepare them to meet the wants of their future career as business men, good citizens, or rulers, it is no less necessary that the education of girls, whose future work, if a comparison be admissible, is higher than man's, be also that which is substantial and which will most fully prepare them for the duties of their sacred office.

Let, therefore, the unjust distinction between boys and girls as regards education be tolerated no longer. Our sons need education no more than do our daughters. The mission of the latter is no less important than that of the former. Any discrimination then in favor of the education of boys in preference to that of girls is not only unwise but also unjust. Both have their work in the world, and both need preparation and training to perform that work properly.

Our systems of education must not discriminate between the rich and the poor. All classes must be admitted to the same privileges. The soul of the rich is no more precious in the sight of the Lord than is that of the poor. The brightest of intellects has often been hid in the body of the most humble. The history of the world's geniuses attests the truth of this. Let us therefore have a full development for every mind, whether embodied in such as are clad in purple and fine linen, or in those surrounded by the extremest and most wretched poverty.

We need education not only for the professional man and the merchant but also for the laboring classes. Educated labor pays. It pays the laborer and it pays the employer. The educated laborer always commands higher wages than the ignorant, and it is most profitable for the employer to have those men work for him who are most intelligent, and who can therefore more fully appreciate and understand his wants. But aside from the pecuniary consideration, universal education has an unlimited influence for good on the moral and mental development of all classes. Volumes of statistics could be cited, were it necessary, to prove that vice and crime are on the side of ignorance.

Let us hope that the day is not distant when all classes shall be educated, when the privileges of education which are now nominally free to all shall be in reality so; when not only our sons but also our daughters, not only merchants and professional men but also mechanics and laborers, shall enjoy equally the advantages of a liberal and substantial education. Then may we hope to establish a government which shall no longer be the plaything of politicians whose gold may buy the ballots of ignorant voters; for all who exercise the right of suffrage shall then vote not according to the dictates of party creed and party leaders but according to the dictates of an untrammelled conscience. We shall then have a government which in grandeur and power shall transcend the grandest conception of the most powerful monarchies on earth.

CHAPTER XXI.

NORMAL DEVELOPMENT.

FOR the want of some better subject as a heading to this chapter, I have adopted that of Normal Development, under which I find it necessary to throw together a number of partially connected thoughts on some of the requisite methods of development, and name some of the qualifications essential in those to whom is intrusted the education and government of the youth of the land. The reader therefore who on opening this volume expects to find a discourse on either Normal Schools or the methods of teaching pursued in those institutions, will be disappointed, as the word normal is here used in its broadest sense as applied to all right education.

The normal development of the child, whether mental, moral, or physical, is the natural method. When we attempt to reverse the natural method and substitute one of our own, we fail; this is inevitable, and it is right too that we should be defeated in our plans when they conflict with those of God. There is a natural method of developing a child's powers of mind, just as there is a natural method of strengthening and developing its physical powers. We wait for its limbs to grow strong before it attempts to stand; it stands for some time before it makes any effort to walk; and we would regard any attempt to teach it to jump or run before it knows how to walk as utter folly. Thus the child's physical powers are strengthened and developed in a natural order which cannot be subverted without injury to its growth and strength. We understand this, and train the child's powers accordingly. Such is, however, not the case in the development of the child's mind. There is here too the same natural order of development, and yet it may be said with truth that there are indeed few who understand this order, and fewer still who in their educating processes take special pains to comply with its demands. Thus in the very outstart we combat the plan which nature dictates, and substitute one of our own. We coop up our children by fifties, sometimes more, in uncomfortable rooms, and set them to learning arbitrary characters which convey to the child's mind no meaning, and thus in the beginning ignore nature's method of development. It is a rare case that the child during the earliest portion of its school-life finds itself going to school eagerly, as it does to the fields or the woods. I would by no means have it understood that it is this wild, frolicking life that the child should lead. Far from it. Unless it is made to feel the controlling influence of a power and will superior to its own, there is but little hope of keeping it within bounds in the future. There is, however, work into which the child enters earnestly, and therefore profitably, long before it is really prepared for school-life. I have in a preceding chapter referred to the proper development of the observing faculties. Here is the starting-point. The change from this pleasant way of acquiring knowledge to that more tedious must be gradual. It is not to be wondered at that pupils frequently do not like their earliest school-days. More of the pleasant should be mingled with the unpleasant. We should pay more attention to the cultivation of the observing faculties by introducing into our primary schools a course of object lessons, and the time of confinement to the schoolroom should be shortened.

In a measure our training is sometimes abnormal, from the fact that we ignore some of the first principles on which all true development rests. One of these has been spoken of in the last paragraph. Another, and the only one to which I shall refer, is, *Opposition as a means of development.* In physical development this principle is acknowledged on all hands, because it comes home to every one's personal experience. We know that to strengthen our bodies we must exercise them. The greater strength of the farmer does not arise from his breathing pure air, though partly owing to this. He grows strong by the labor he performs. His muscles become round, full, and rigid, according to the amount of healthful exercise to which he subjects them. Thus, too, the vocalist and the elocutionist strengthen and develop their vocal organs by daily practice, preparing themselves to overcome one difficulty by surmounting another. The same principle holds good in mental and moral development. From the moment our minds begin to develop, they are strengthened by the opposition which they must necessarily overcome. It is an unwise policy then that leads us to help children over difficulties which they can surmount without assistance. Difficulties will necessarily arise, and it is not the part of either teacher or parent to manifest an improper eagerness and haste to remove them so long as they are not of such a character as to baffle the child's efforts. Each victory gained but helps to strengthen the child, and the more bitter the struggle the sweeter the fruits of victory. In moral training too the same principles should govern us. Each temptation resisted and each act of self-denial practised makes the child all the stronger and better able to resist such temptations as may rise in the future.

It is a fact worthy of notice that while there has been much discussion on school-government and methods of teaching, there has been as yet but little discussion with regard to the relative value of the different kinds of knowledge. It is a question on which educators seem extremely sensitive. The graduate of the literary school lays great stress on the languages; calling those who do not believe with him utilitarians and men who cannot comprehend the profundity of thought which characterized the days of heathen deities and gods. The alumni of the scientific school, on the other hand, hold that too much time is given to languages and too little to the "culture demanded by the times," calling their opponents old fogies. Both are jealous of the position their opponents hold, and both in the heat of argument say too much in favor of their special culture. It is not my province here to advocate the dogmas of either party, but is it not a matter of some importance to know the bearing which useful knowledge has on normal culture?

The great arguments of both schools rest on this. Each claims that his course of study is most useful either as a discipline or from its own inherent value. It is, then, important to every one that the relative value of different kinds of knowledge be settled, that we may at once pursue the study of that which is most useful, and thus best calculated to meet all the ends of a true normal development.

I know no better way of closing this chapter, and with it the book, than by saying briefly a few words to parents and teachers with regard to their qualifications for governing and educating children, and of the reward in store for those who do their work well. First, then, they must feel a personal interest in the work. It is scarcely credible that there are those among parents who do not feel a deep, abiding interest in the proper culture of their children, and yet, strange as it may seem, there are such. And how many are there too who take little if any thought for the welfare of their children; who never for a moment stop to think what vicious influence their example may have! And of teachers, of how many may it be said that salary and rest from physical toil are not the strongest motives that lead them to adopt the profession? Would that parents would take a deeper interest in the development of their children, and that teachers too would feel at all times the unlimited power they have for good in assisting this development.

Those who are engaged in this good work will meet with many trials. Children at best are but poor, frail mortals, our own miniatures, and we need to be charitable to their faults and shortcomings. Day after day they may be guilty of little acts of indiscretion which are annoying to those having them in charge; but with the exercise of patience, we can overcome all these. No one needs greater patience than the teacher and the parent.

Lastly, we must be prayerful. Any system of education, as I have before said, which attempts without God's help to produce fruit, is and must be vicious, it matters not what its name. God, the head and source of creation, must here also be the source from which we seek help and guidance. The man who is not a believer in God is dangerous everywhere, but nowhere more so than in the family or the school-room as the guide and governor of children. See to it, parents, that you set an example here too for your children which shall not only be worthy of imitation, but which shall direct and lead your little ones to the Saviour, who has so beautifully said, "Suffer little children to come unto me, and forbid them not, for of such is the kingdom of Heaven."

Is not the reward ample? Who does not experience a feeling of satisfaction when he finds himself the doer of a good deed or the performer of a good act? How much greater pride may we feel in ourselves and in our work if we train up our children aright! But this is not the only reward. The gratitude of our children in after life, the influence we exercise for good on society, and the praise we receive for our good work, are each a sufficient reward for the toil we may undergo. Add to these the crown with which Christ shall bedeck the brow of the faithful, and the hope of meeting in a world of bliss to come all those who under our guidance and instruction, with the assistance of God, have attained an eternal inheritance with the angels, and whose lutes join with ours in praising the great Jehovah, and is not our measure full to overflowing? Think of it, parents and teachers, are not the pure love of a crucified Saviour and the approving smile of a just and all-wise God more than we could ask? And yet we shall have these. Enter into the work then prayerfully, and let us by wise and proper culture aim to produce a generation of well-developed men and women, who shall be an honor to their Maker and living monuments of His love, and grace, and beauty; and when we come to have sentence passed upon us, may it be said, "Well done, good and faithful servant; thou hast been faithful over a few things, I will make thee ruler over many things; enter thou into the joy of thy Lord."

THE END.

www.ingramcontent.com/pod-product-compliance
Lightning Source LLC
LaVergne TN
LVHW011204110826
845150LV00006B/1314

* 9 7 8 1 4 2 5 5 1 8 2 1 9 *